Falling in *love* works ***better*** than **PROZAC!**

Falling in love works better than PROZAC!

Jessica R. Gera

BURMANBOOKS

Copyright © 2010 Falling in Love Works Better than Prozac!

Published by BurmanBooks Inc.
260 Queens Quay West
Suite 904
Toronto, Ontario
Canada M5J 2N3

All rights reserved. No part of this publication may be reproduced, stored in a retrieval system, or transmitted in any form by any process—electronic, photocopying, recording, or otherwise—without the prior written consent of BurmanBooks Inc.

Cover and interior design:
Jack Steiner

Editing:
Drew Tapley

Distribution:
Trumedia Group
c/o Ingram Publisher Services
14 Ingram Blvd.
LaVergne, TN 37086

ISBN 978-1-897404-31-7

Printed and bound in Canada

Dedicated to three generations of lovin':

My grandmother, Bimla Gupta
My mother, Sudha Gera
My sister, Mainika Singla

For all those folks who have ever "broke," and *chose* **to put themselves back together again.**

Contents

Part 1:
Mountain Climbing

Mountain Climbers.................... 2
Bruised, Broken 'n' Bitter vs. Better......... 3
Who Am I Anyway?.................... 4
Real................................. 6
Bruised & Broken..................... 7
Sweaters............................. 10
Black Cat at a Wedding 15
The Bitter Club: Invitation Rejected 17
The Better Club 21
The Mountain Gets Bigger............. 22
Pain................................. 23
21cm 29
Cancer 32
Decision Time: Bitter or Better?.......... 38
Five Requests 48
Thank Your Lucky Scars.............. 51
Better Better Better!................. 53
Today 55
The View From Up Top 62

Part 2:
The Bitter Battlefield

RSVP 68
Be Wary of Bitter: It Can Disguise
    Itself 71
Getting Better: Your Health 72
Healing and Forgiveness: Find Your
    Magic Wand 79
Falling in Love Works Better Than
    Prozac 91
One Final Pet Peeve 98

Preface

Dear readers, I come to you with a plea. You see, there is an epidemic spreading like wildfire all across the globe, and I need you to help me stop it. I warn you, this is a tough battle, but I am very confident that if we all come together, we will come out victorious. I promise that I won't just send you out to battle without protecting you. Just like any prepared warrior, you will have all the necessary tools you need in order to stop... *them*. They're dangerous. They're sneaky. They're growing. But most importantly, they're *bitter*.

At this very moment they're recruiting and preying on young and impressionable minds, people who lack support systems, and people who are struggling in trying times. It is *our* mission to stop them by providing them with the same tools that I am about to give to you.

Here is your mission:

1. Learn how to use your tools in Part One.
2. Learn how to use your tools in Part Two.
3. Find them: The Bruised, Broken 'n' *Bitter* Club.
4. Introduce yourself: The Bruised, Broken 'n' *Better* Club.
5. Pass on your knowledge of how falling in love works better than Prozac.

Preface

    I have complete faith in all of you to carry out your mission successfully.
    Remember, be safe. They've been bitter for a long time. DO NOT let them sway you.

    I wish you well in your journey.

With love,

Jessica
Proud member of The Bruised, Broken 'n' Better Club
Accepting new members at all times

PART 1:
Mountain Climbing

Mountain Climbers

My challenge to myself and to you is to continuously climb the mountain that you are on no matter how tired you become, and no matter what gets thrown at you along the way.

I get it. It's much easier said than done. But what isn't? I have no idea what mountain you're on, and don't pretend to understand your specific challenges, your hurdles or your heartaches. I can only tell you what I do know: that the mountain I've climbed has been anything but small. In fact, it was enormous, and seemed to grow bigger and bigger with each day that passed. I do know that over the years, I climbed and climbed yet never really felt like I was anywhere near the top. I was wrong.

Along the way I had to choose to keep climbing—or jump off, give up, accept defeat, and wallow in self-pity. And let me tell you, jumping off with the knowledge that I'd land on my face with a big fat splat, still sounded like an appealing option. It was just easier. But it wasn't my style; and I bet that it isn't yours either.

In my journey, I've met many other mountain climbers who knew just how challenging and exhausting their climb was going to be, and they accepted it.

They just kept climbing. No complaining, no bitching, no making excuses along the way. I also met those who liked to speak of their climb in every step they took, and complained that those around them were comfortably strolling in the park on a perfect summer's day. Their eyes looked green with envy; their posture locked in a boxer's stance.

Both types of climbers were sad. Both were hurting. One would eventually get to the top and bask in the pride and accomplishment of climbing the mother of all mountains. The other would climb one baby step at a time, moaning and groaning the entire way while other climbers would slowly pass them by.

One *chose* to do everything in their power to get *better*. The other settled for being *bitter*.

Bruised, Broken 'n' Bitter vs. Better

We'll all climb our own mountains in life, and at some point we'll get bruised. Maybe the cute girl with the pigtails in kindergarten didn't give you the time of day? Then, you'll get broken. Something you worked your hardest at didn't turn out the way you wanted it to. You lost your job after a decade of being with the same company. Someone broke your heart. Your kids hurt you. Your parents hurt you. The person you expected more from turned their back on you.

Then comes the decision of all decisions, the most important decision you will ever have to make in your entire life: to get bitter or get better.

Who Am I Anyway?

I think I need to make a couple of things crystal clear right from the very beginning. I do this thing a lot. Some refer to it as "eccentric charm," some may know it better as sarcasm. I like to refer to it as "healthy sarcasm".

Never confuse sarcasm with negativity. Sarcasm, when delivered correctly, makes people smile; and when delivered superbly can even make people laugh. I would like nothing more than for all of us to do just that—laugh at ourselves, laugh out loud, and laugh wholeheartedly. You will see many sides of me in this book, but foremost, I am a firm believer that you can speak the truth without being a jerk. Being able to be completely straightforward and still come off well isn't easy. I've seen many folks try and end up offending almost everyone in the room. It's not an easy skill, but if you care enough to master it, you most certainly will.

I have tremendous respect for those who practice the balancing act between honesty and heart-a truly rare find.

When the concept was first presented to me to write a "self help" book, I must admit that I snickered. I didn't snicker at self-help books; I snickered at the concept of me writing one! So, it began with a snicker, and then transformed into hysterical laughter—the belly aching kind of laughter that takes you a good five to seven minutes to calm down from. Then, just when you do, you lock eye contact with someone and burst into hysterics all over again. We've all been there. Except this time, when I looked around to make eye contact, no one else laughed with me. Everyone seemed to think it was a wonderful idea. In fact, the people that I love the most, the people that know me, *really* know me the most, took this opportunity to tell me why they thought I should definitely take on this project. They reminded me of that mountain climb.

I had absolutely no intention of speaking about my personal life to any of you. The plan was simply to write a book about life and provide my readers with some life experience skills that I picked up along the way—the same life experience skills that truly brought me to a very happy and healthy place. So I submitted just that to my editor who very quickly made me realize that the book had zero substance. He didn't say it like that, he was very nice about it, but really, this was the message. I battled him on it. Ultimately, I learned that he was right.

I told him I had no intention of speaking about my life with anyone. He repeatedly asked me why, and I really didn't have any good answers. I learned that I was hesitant in doing this because of what people would say. I decided that after everything I'd seen in my life, fearing gossip is now just as scary to me as a really cheesy '80s horror film. I learned that while some may still dramatically scream at each scene, most have moved on to better films.

The reality is that I don't have a PhD, I haven't invented anything, and I'm not a self-made millionaire. So I guess I can't expect any of you to take my "life advice" seriously without knowing who I am, what I've seen, and where I come from. I accept that. Fair enough.

Real

Some people subscribe to a religion, some to political ideologies, some to really weird cults that mess with your head. To each their own. While I do have my own religious beliefs, I also subscribe to something else that keeps me grounded—the concept of *real*. I believe and practice it in every step of my life.

Being real means speaking directly from the heart, without any bullshit; and that takes courage. It means knowing that, at some point or another, everyone falls. Sometimes, we fall multiple times. As human beings, we fall. We break. And guess what? It's *okay* to fall. It's *great* to fall. And it's *great* to get broken.

You will see later in this book that I encourage everyone to "get broken" at least once in their lives. How strong you are is irrelevant, and so is how much you've been through.

I don't discount the importance of positivity, but it really irks me when many allude to the fact that they just persevered until they got to where they wanted to. Just like that, all folded up in a neat little pile of positive thinking and perseverance with a fat, juicy cherry on top. It doesn't quite work that way, and I'll challenge anyone on that notion.

It's actually more like this: You got really upset, you got really ticked off, and then you relied on family and friends and all of their support; you picked yourself up off your ass and remembered all the things you should be grateful for. And then, and only then, did you get to where you wanted to go.

Sometimes, you fall all over again, but as time passes with every life obstacle, you still get upset, but it doesn't seem to last as long as it used to. You feel stronger, and you're going to get better and better at this every single time life throws something your way. You're human, and you're *allowed* to get upset.

You get bruised. You get broken. You get upset. Then you *choose* to get better.

Now that's real.

Bruised & Broken

The first time I ever got *bruised* was when I was seven years old and my father suffered a severe heart attack, leaving him with symptoms very similar to Parkinson's disease. I had no idea what that meant at the time. All I knew was that he was ill, and maybe he would get better soon. But as time went on, I began to clue in, *really* clue in, as to what was going on. He wasn't getting better.

A man who was notorious for being on the go at all

times could no longer feed himself, go up and down the stairs, drive a car, or even go to the bathroom on his own. When you're a child, your father is a superhero. They take care of you, nurture you, and guide you. They knock down those mountains so that your climb is that much easier. He wasn't able to do that. It wasn't his fate. He was ill, and there wasn't a damn thing that any doctor could do to fix him. When I put that reality together in my mind, I *broke*. Something inside of me broke, and stayed broken for a very long time.

I remember that time of my life very clearly. I grew into my teen years and no longer felt like a child. Quite frankly, there was no time to be a child. My mom had to take care of our finances, two daughters, and her husband. All I knew was that I wanted to make life easier for everyone that I loved most. I helped feed my father, I helped him to go the washroom, go up and down the stairs, and I helped him lie down on the couch. I mowed the lawn, shovelled the snow, and cleaned up whenever and wherever I could. I did this knowing that most kids in my class were playing video games, hop scotching, or were at Disneyland. They were being kids.

I parented my parent before I got to finish being a kid, and I grew up quick. It was no one's fault. It's what life had dealt, and it was damn hard. As much as it "wasn't fair," I'm glad I did it. As I fed my dad chicken noodle soup, he would look at me and say, "Thank you for feeding me and always trying to help me." It wasn't the first time his eyes had filled up with tears as he thanked me for taking care of him. I'll never forget those moments, sacrificing being a kid in order to help take care of him. It was the hardest thing I've ever done in my life, and he knew it. He would talk to me about that sometimes.

He was proud of me for all I had done for him, and while I didn't know it then, the mere knowledge that my dad was proud of who I was has now given me back everything that I had "lost." I never got to see him as my superhero, but if I was able to be one to him, even for just a split second, then all the sacrifices were well worth it.

I was fifteen years old when my father died. My family had watched his illness deteriorate for eight years, and although I pride myself on being a pretty good writer, I absolutely cannot describe the feeling of watching your parent's health deteriorate right in front of your eyes; much less through the eyes of a young child. I was left without the guidance of a father in the midst of other young kids who all seemed to have two parents at home, and that broke me all over again. Years later, I see that I was left with a relationship between a grandmother, mother, and sister that would grow to levels of strength and *love* I didn't know were possible. I'm thankful for this every single day of my life.

Low self-esteem combined with needing to grow up quicker than I anticipated left me socially awkward. My mentality was definitely different, and I found that I didn't really fit in with anyone in my own age group. My mind was usually filled with responsibilities that needed to be fulfilled today, and preparing myself for responsibilities that would need to be fulfilled tomorrow.

Without really having any friends around in my childhood that weren't busy with their own families, it got pretty lonely. Although I was still showered with love and affection from my entire family, I still felt a void, and when school was out, it was like the clock didn't move. That's when my two greatest loves were born. I immersed myself in every book I could get a hold of. You know your mind is on a different level than your peers when you're sympathizing with a thirty-five-year-old character in a book before your sixteenth birthday. I also fell in love with music. I learned to listen, and I learned to learn.

I taped every music video of every artist that I loved (yes "taped" as in VHS; I wasn't born into the DVD era) and *fell in love* with the sound, the words and the passion from each song and each composer. *I fell in love* with their talent. Oddly, I had no idea at the time that I fell in love with anything. It just seemed like writing, reading and music were my favourite hobbies. They weren't hobbies—they were far more than that; but I would only make that connection later on.

Sweaters

Years later, I got married. Three and a half years after that, I got divorced. I *broke* again.

My family taught me that life was not just filled with butterflies and roses. Once you had truly earned it, you could stop and play with those butterflies, and stop to smell those roses. But first, you had to work for it. You had to earn it; and the same is true for marriage.

When I heard others speak of their marriages, and subsequent divorces, it was like they were speaking about a really great sweater they had once bought. This sweater definitely stood out, and they just had to have it. Without trying it on for size and making sure it was a good fit, they made the purchase; but before leaving the store they were sure to ask the salesperson, "Erm, this is returnable... right?" The answer? "Exchanges only."

I guess that when I bought *my* sweater, I saw it as the last sweater in the world I would ever buy. I never really cared about shopping around, and the concept of it being returnable didn't cross my mind.

Have you ever seen those people who wear sweaters that don't quite fit them? It's like they're stuffing their bodies into a sweater that's way too tiny for them, or they're drowning in a sweater that's way too large. Either way, it's not a pretty picture. Then of course, through years of wearing it, it stretches out here and there, or it shrinks through runs in the dryer. Although they've always known that it was never really their size, it's become *good enough. It'll do.*

Those sweaters are what they're used to. Taking them off would just make them feel naked, embarrassed, and send them out shopping all over again. So instead, they decided to pull, pry or shrink those sweaters until they somehow fit their bodies.

I didn't want that. I wanted a good fit. Not a perfect fit—a good fit. A healthy fit. And besides, I really didn't feel like ruining a sweater that would probably just look better on someone else.

When my decision was made, my mother and sister looked me dead straight in the eye and said, "You're going to be happy after this is all over, and we're there with you every step of the way." And they were.

I am not an advocate of divorce, but I most certainly am an advocate of happiness, good health and love. Simply walking away before putting in every last effort will just bring you to another really neat—and seasonal—sweater. Just wanted to make that clear.

Déjà Vu

The aftermath of a divorce is a mountain climb in itself. I hope that you'll never have to experience this for yourself, but if you have climbed that very same mountain then you don't need an explanation from me.

I did a lot of reflecting during this time and, almost instinctively, grabbed the first book in sight, feeling the same comfort that I had sought out during childhood. I read absolutely everything I could get a hold of from fiction to non-fiction, magazine and newspaper articles, medical journals, Internet blogs and trashy entertainment scandals. I read and read, and read, and fell in love with reading all over again. I fell in love with the art of story.

Toward the end of my marriage, I published my very first online article. I was so proud of it. It was really small-time stuff, and I was well aware of that, but seeing my article posted up on someone's website with the headline, "By: Jessica R. Gera," gave me a sense of accomplishment that I thought could never be matched. I decided that there was no time like the present to continue that writing. It would keep me focused, and it would keep my mind occupied from thinking about things that only made me feel terrible. In simplest terms, it put me on the route to getting better.

Every time I picked up my favourite lead pencil and old notebook, I felt a sensation of happiness that was just foreign to me. I couldn't believe how much I absolutely loved to write. I submitted articles to magazines, associations, organizations, charities and businesses, and ended up publishing fourteen articles in less than a year. It felt wonderful.

Whenever I had a severe case of writer's block, I would quote Hip Hop stars, '80s divas, Rock 'n' Roll legends, and just about any tune in any genre to illustrate a point in my articles, even in my daily conversations. In simplest terms, music made me feel magnificent. The words, the beat, the artist and the producer, made blood rush through my body at warp speed.

Falling in love with *something* made me choose better over bitter. There was no time, no space in my life to get bitter. Whenever I was feeling down, the things that I absolutely loved brought me back to a happy and healthy place. It didn't happen overnight, it took time. But I got there.

I just kept climbing.

My Community & Culture to the Rescue

After going through a healthy grieving process and coming to terms with my divorce, it was time to get back out there and live my life. I had incorrectly assumed two major hurdles.

I thought about meeting men and having to explain *why* I was divorced. I'd have to prove that there was nothing wrong with me, and show them that I really am mentally stable! So not only was I fretting before every date, I was also worried about being judged by my elders and people I respected in my own community. I worried I'd be labelled as *that girl* who "didn't know the value of marriage," and "gave up." I worried about being judged.

I was surprised to find that none of the men I met made me feel inadequate or unwanted because I was divorced, and I thought that was damn cool. The elders in my community genuinely reminded me that they knew my heart; they knew me and were there to support me no matter what. I was overcome with emotion, and realized that I really should have given them more credit.

So if these weren't my hurdles, then what was in store for me?

Black Cat at a Wedding

Some did judge, and some were scared by my mere presence.

I was invited to a wedding ceremony after my divorce. I wasn't very close to the bride and groom, but we were acquaintances, and I was happy to share in their special day. In a Hindu wedding, we use a scarf to tie the garments from both the bride and groom as they embark on their seven circles of promise and love. The scarf that literally and metaphorically ties the couple together is done to symbolize their never-ending bond and commitment. So you could imagine the disappointment both bride and groom would feel if that knot wasn't tied tight enough. It would be equivalent to the part in a Christian marriage when the priest asks, "If anyone present opposes this marriage, speak now or forever hold your peace"—and then some fool shouts out, "I oppose it! I oppose it!"

Whoever had tied the knot that day hadn't made it as tight as it should have been, and I could see it loosening. I gasped and stepped forward to prevent a very preventable and unfortunate accident. Others began to notice at the same time that I did, and two of us stepped forward from the audience to re-tie the knot. As I moved toward the couple, a lady looked at me and said, "Oh, not *you*. It's okay. She can do it instead," pointing to the other girl. I stopped in my tracks. *Nooo Jessica, don't be silly!* I said to myself.

Maybe the other girl was just standing closer. There couldn't possibly be any other reason why she wouldn't want me to touch their life-tying knot, right?

Wrong. My heart sank, and it hurt. I knew I didn't deserve that kind of bullshit. No one does.

That's the thing: this lady knew it too. She basically told me to refrain from touching anything because I may pass on the fate of a divorce (talk about a whole different kind of Midas touch!). Later on, the same woman came to speak to me, awkwardly and repeatedly, throughout the night. I don't even think she knew my name, but she knew what she had done. After continuously asking me if I'd like something to drink (when there was a drink in my hand), or if I wanted something to eat (while I was chewing on my food), I knew that she was sorry, ashamed, and felt guilty. I forgave her. She had grown up in a different time, as part of a different generation, with superstitions that would always get the better of some of them. I wish I could say the same about women my own age.

Good Indian Girls

Good Indian girls don't get divorced, eh? I never thought of being East Indian as something I'd have to prove. It's simply something I am. My identity. My pride. Trying to take it away from me is as easy as knockin' Jay-Z off his empire. It's not gonna happen.

Indian culture is beautiful, heartfelt and intelligent. I'm proud to have been born into it, yet I feel a sense of sorrow for those unfortunate folks who misunderstand the true meaning of our culture.

The Bitter Clubs: Invitation Rejected

It didn't cross my mind that I would be judged by my peers. These people didn't make up the majority of my peer group in my community, but they were out there. I'd like to introduce you to a few groups of women.

The Brown Stepford Wives Club suffers from a very unique disease. I call it the "Culturally Confused Syndrome." For whatever reason, these women believe that those who are not married by a certain age, those that are married and don't have any children by a certain time, those that are divorced, those that are separated, and those that are gay—are actually committing some sort of cultural injustice. The fact that they are married (happily or not) makes them believe that they occupy a higher social status on their culturally confused hierarchy. (A hierarchy that exists only in their eeny weeny teeny minds.) So, you could imagine their reaction when they found out I was now divorced.

Whatever happened to just wanting to see someone find a life partner for the sole sake of their own happiness? It shocks me that some of these highly educated people could not put together the notion that maybe the object of their judgment was not in their particular position by choice. Geez, I'd love to smack just one of them. Okay, maybe two of them.

So, how do you become a member of the Brown Stepford Wives Club? Well, first off, you need to be married to a brown man. (That would be my first strike.) Second, you absolutely must have the ability to stare for at least 4½ minutes without blinking, and feel a sense of sick pleasure in making this person feel as uncomfortable as humanly possible. (Strike two).

Third, you must absolutely have no interest in speaking of anything besides what your husband does, what he makes, what he drives, who he knows, what his parents do, how much they make, what they drive, who they know... repeat for all family members, distant cousins and prominent family friends. In short, you must present yourself as someone who holds a weird and slightly sick crush, as opposed to someone who is blessed with a life partner. (Strike three.)

How did I become such an expert on the ins and outs of the Brown Stepford Wives Club? Well, I got the invite back when I was married. I wasn't interested then, and I ain't interested now.

The second group of women are not yet a part of the Brown Stepford Wives Club, but have submitted their application six weeks before the deadline. They really want in. These women are attached to brown men who hold a decent job, look decent, and belong to decent families; but it was never good enough. These wannabe Brown Stepfords always want more in terms of status, wealth and buff. These couples were wearing the wrong size sweaters right from the beginning, and every time I've witnessed one of those decent men ripping off that sweater, I've had to fight the urge to stand up with a megaphone in-hand and scream, "Good for you decent brown man! Good for you!"

A lot of the women in this group may not have been my best friends, but they were a part of my life in some way. They all changed their tunes very quickly after I got divorced, and I must admit to feeling *bruised* by that. The same women who once wanted to go grab a bite to eat, go shopping, or just hang out; well, apparently something happened to their phones. Apparently, they all had some sort of technical problem that just coincidently occurred at the same time as my divorce. Those damn cell phone companies!

After a while, this group became more of a source of entertainment than an annoyance. That's when I met the third group, which I aptly called "The We Hate All Brown Men Club." Geez, why was everyone such an extremist?

While the previous two clubs idolized their husbands or boyfriends to a level of eerie, greed, and insecurity (as opposed to genuine love and commitment), the other club seemed to bash all men at every opportunity they got. These women scared me even more than watching a horror movie, by myself, on a rainy night, as the power goes out, while dolls start talking to me… and then someone comes knockin' at the door. I felt that in order to fit in with them, I would have to show up at their next gathering with some poor brown guy's head on a stick and chant some weird kind of Voodoo jibber jabber while I ferociously flapped my arms in the air. It just wasn't for me. But nonetheless, I got the invite from them too. In fact, each group called out to me like a really cheesy "say no to drugs" after-school special, and I'm proud of myself for just saying NO!

Anyway, after deciding that all three groups of women scared me more than Eminem's diss to Mariah Carey, I decided to steer clear of all of them. While each group was different in their own unique and ridiculously weird way, they all shared one thing in common (besides the insistent staring). They were all bitter—but something tells me they didn't start out that way.

I would bet anything that the first group of women, The Brown Stepford Wives Club, began as very lonely women who, over time, found one another. They were all married to prominent and affluent men (or men who lied about being prominent or affluent), who unfortunately spent no time with their wives. What started off as loneliness turned into something else over time. Their innocence in loneliness at the beginning, transformed itself into bitterness over the years; a transformation that they *allowed* to happen. They *allowed* negative feelings to fester, which is a really, really dangerous move because ultimately, those negative feelings take over your identity. And that's when you become bitter. Correction. That's when you *choose* to become bitter.

This was the first time in my life I had ever really seen what bitter looked like, and I swore that I would never allow myself to walk down that path. While I may poke fun at some of these folks, I genuinely do feel a sense of sorrow for them. They should know that they're welcome into the "better" club at any time should they decide to jump ship.

The Better Club

I truly have some exceptional friends. I adore them and love them. Blood may be thicker than water, but I have some stand up women in my life who truly make that notion questionable. (They know exactly who they are.) They climbed with me very step of the way, and I'd be nothing without them. These were the people that I really wanted to spend time with more than anyone else, so I joined their club—a club that always chooses better over bitter.

It looked like life was getting back to normal again. The divorce was slowly sinking its way into my past, and I was excited about building a brand new future. Comments and judgments went right over my head quicker than a joke told to Brittany Spears. I didn't get it, I didn't care to get it, and it didn't bug me that I didn't get it.

I was in awe of so many successful and wonderful people I had met along the way; people who were involved in so many outstanding projects. I was excited about new friendships, travel, work, exercise, seeing new movies, dating, and living my brand new and wonderful life. Maybe it was okay that childhood had been the way it was. Maybe it was okay that the divorce happened. Maybe I really didn't have "bad luck". This was my fate, and now it looked like I could wipe the slate clean. It looked like things were starting to look up. Finally, I could start over. Finally, I could catch a break!

Not so fast Jessica. Not so fast...

The Mountain Gets Bigger

It seemed that the same mountain I had been climbing for years and years had somehow, miraculously, grown bigger. With no warning, with no apologies, with no rhyme or reason, it extended itself higher and higher up into the sky.

Two years after my divorce, I was diagnosed with ovarian cancer. I was twenty-nine years old.

I remember the day I got diagnosed very clearly, and people always ask me, "Jess, what was going through your mind?" Well, more than anything, I was thinking about every step of that mountain climb that I had walked to date. I mean, this was no bunny hill. It was starting to feel like I was climbing Mount Everest.

I felt like I had been struggling, working and sweating since I was seven years old. And then I started thinking about how my mom and my grandmother always told me to: "Acknowledge your fate! Embrace your destiny! Speak to your spirituality!"

So, to answer the question as to what was going through my mind: "My fate. My destiny. My spirituality."

I told them all to fuck off. That's about as *real* an answer that I can give you.

Pain

I knew something was up. I had known for a while. I just didn't have a clue that it would be so severe.

Ever seen a treasure troll? They're those little dolls that people think are really cute, but in fact they're actually quite ugly. They have those little jewels in their bellybutton. They're built with a normal body, and then have this little belly that just pops right out like a pregnant child. Seriously, what marketing department came up with this concept?

Every time I would eat even the lightest meal, my stomach would do just that. Instantly, it would pop right out like a pregnant woman in her first trimester. I noticed it again and again, and realized I had a severe bloating issue. At first, I chalked it up to it being around that wonderful time of the month where we women get to cramp, cry and cuss. Over time, though, I realized that the bloating was happening both on and off my cycle. My pants were no longer fitting properly on Monday, but then on Tuesday they would fit again. It was the most bizarre thing I had ever seen my body do.

I was always that girl who had really bad cramps around my time of the month, but over the years it had gotten progressively worse. I couldn't walk because of a pain in my lower abdomen that was so severe I had to immediately stop what I was doing. My hot water bottle became my new BFF. This is how I spent my time for a long time—bloating, cramps, can't walk, clothes don't fit, have to lie down, pain, pain, pain... and then it would go away. Then it would come back.

A lower back pain would kick in. It usually started off feeling like someone had placed big weights on my lower back and decided to leave them there to sit and hang out for a while. Over time, it started to feel like those same weights were being whipped against my lower back by some really strong, tough weightlifter guy. I promise you, this time, I'm not being sarcastic. It hurt like a bitch.

I didn't lift anything heavy. My job doesn't require me to engage in physical labour, and I wasn't engaging in any sort of raw and crazy sex either! So what was up with my lower back? It was time to get an answer from the doctor, and he went through many scenarios. I was told I needed orthotics. After six months the pain didn't go away. Regular massage therapy for another six months. The pain didn't go away. Perhaps I was just mentally stressed out from the events of the last few, er... twenty-nine years. Now, this was the kicker.

There was no doubt that I'd had an "eventful" life, but I could tell that every medical practitioner I visited was far more interested in my stress levels than the actual symptoms I was complaining about. It got to the point where I really started to question my own sanity. When several doctors are telling you that "it's in your head," you start to believe them. And I did believe them, for a little while. As days passed, the pain was getting more and more severe. I felt helpless, and no longer knew what was making me feel worse: The fact that I was in serious physical pain, or that no one seemed to be able to diagnose it? Or was it the fact that I was told I was imagining it! I'd say the latter pissed me off the most.

I would think about it all the time, and it would consume my every thought. Why did I feel so awful? Why was I in so much pain, and when would it stop? Would it ever stop? Was I really just making this all up in my mind? Am I losing my mind? No, I'm not! Why won't anyone believe me?

I would make plans to go out with my family and friends to see a new flick, go for a drink, go for dinner, or even go on vacation—but it never really worked out. I'd get up in the morning with a pain so severe I felt like a knife was stabbing through my stomach and lower back, over and over again. There was nothing I could do but simply endure it; and so I did, deciding I'd just have to live with it.

I was out of options, and was wearing my orthotics from the time I woke up in the morning to the time I went to sleep at night, regardless of whether I left my house or not. I engaged in regular massage therapy even though it never really made me feel any better.

And so I lived with it for a while, and went back to living my life. None of the doctors I spoke to really seemed to take me seriously… until one day.

Most Memorable Date

Going into the last week of May 2009, I loved every moment of living in the condo I had rented with one of my best friends for the summer. Committed to keeping an open mind on the dating scene, I went out on a date with a very decent guy. The plans were always the same: Meet up for a coffee or a drink, and engage in some chit chat and get to know each other a bit better. The standard stuff. As I was getting dressed to go out, my right side was aching. I didn't understand it, but quite frankly, I didn't care anymore. I was sick of feeling pain, emotionally and now physically, and decided to ignore it, convinced it would go away. It didn't.

As I finished getting ready for my date, the pangs got sharper. When I slipped on my favourite heals, the pain sharpened even more. I barked the address to my cab driver, and felt a gut wrenching pain so severe I didn't know what else to do but just put my head back and rest until I got to the restaurant. It was getting stronger and stronger on the furthest right side of my abdomen, twisting and turning like a knife plunging its way into my body. This time, it wasn't your standard kitchen knife, more like one of those big butcher's knives.

It'll go away, it'll go away, I told myself while concentrating on the people in the street through the cab window. I remember wondering to myself if any of these random strangers that I was passing had ever felt a pain like this before. If so, what did their doctors tell them? Was it in their imagination too? Am I going crazy? A text message from my date interrupted my thoughts. He was apologizing for running about twenty minutes late. *Perfect!* I thought to myself. I'll just splash some water on my face and I'll be good to go. I opened the taxi door, extended my right foot down onto the ground, stood up, and... BANG!

I have never felt anything like that in my entire life. It's a real struggle to try and describe what I felt, but I'll give it my best shot. It was like being cut by the sharpest knife used by the most inelegant and ungraceful hands. Moreover, it felt like it was being done by someone with intensive anger management issues; with no painkillers, and no anesthetic.

The pain that started on the right side of my lower stomach began banging against my right hip bone. Then it would shoot up again back to the right side of my abdomen. What began as a feeling of being cut now turned into a stabbing sensation—harder, and then harder into my skin. I wasn't only overcome with pain; I was overcome with shock and fear. What was happening to me?

It took everything in me to not scream. I almost hit the floor. The right side of my stomach was now on fire like someone had lit a match to the right side of my body. Sweat poured from head to toe, and I felt weak. Convinced that I was about to hit the pavement, I threw a $20 bill at the cab driver for my $8 cab ride, and took off to the nearest restroom. Guess it was his lucky day. It most certainly wasn't mine.

In the bathroom of the restaurant I couldn't stand up—sitting, squatting, lying down on the disgusting floor begging and pleading for the pain to "please-please-please-please stop." I know what you're thinking. Why didn't I call an ambulance? Go to the hospital? I struggle with trying to answer that question. After being told several times that my life was "very stressful," and it was perfectly normal for me to "imagine things," I really was starting to believe it.

My mind was racing. *Was I having a stroke? A heart attack? Could it be my kidneys? It's my appendix! It has to be! Maybe even an anxiety attack? Perhaps I was doing this all to myself in panic mode?*

I leaned against the bathroom door on my knees and had absolutely no idea what to do. Twenty minutes later, the pain was gone. Just like that.

Fed Up

My date arrived and ordered a vodka mixer while I ordered a cup of tea, even though I would have been very happy to dull the pain with something stronger. I just figured I should let whatever had happened pass through me before I touched any alcohol. We sat down and chatted for about twenty minutes before it came back. The sweating kicked in, and the pain was back with more vengeance than anything Eminem has ever released.

I got up. "I'm sorry" was really all I could get out. "I'm not well and I have to go." He said, "Um, okay. If you're not interested just say so." I looked back at him and realized he was just joking. He sincerely looked worried and told me he hoped I felt better soon. I didn't have the energy to open my mouth and speak, and just jumped into a cab and went back to my condo to explain to my best friend what had happened. We sat on the couch together and watched television while she repeatedly told me not to worry, and that she was with me. Over time, the pain went away again.

I woke up the next morning unsure if I had just been attacked. My right side felt like a very-big-strong-wrestler-like man had just beat the hell out of me, pummelling the right side of my abdomen. I literally crawled out of my bed like a toddler, and banged on my friend's bedroom door. "Take me to the hospital. I'm done," I said through clenched teeth. "I don't care what they say. This isn't in my fucking imagination."

21cm

The average size of a cyst in a woman's body is approximately 5cm. I had a 21cm cyst inside me.

I knew something was up when they did an ultrasound and the technician looked at the screen and called a doctor. That doctor called another doctor, and they both just kind of stared at me for a bit. (Ah, back to the staring!) "What?" I screamed out. I had had enough. This pain had been on and off for the last couple of years, and I was so incredibly sick of having to endure it. "Just tell me what it is!" They explained that I had a very large cyst, and that it was quite uncommon and would have to be removed. I hadn't been for surgery since I was six years old and had my tonsils out.

I listen to the doctors. "A cyst? 21cm?" I had a cyst longer than the size of my nephew at the time. How the fuck did I grow that? Then it crossed my mind with the same seriousness as a non-committal relationship: *Could this be cancerous?* It was a random thought; one that I didn't actually believe for a second, but had to ask them anyway.

"I can't say anything for sure Jessica, but I will tell you that for your age and your medical history, it is highly unlikely. There would be a one in a million chance."

If I'm nothing else, then I truly am one in a million.

Hospital Admissions

I was admitted into the hospital, and while it was the first time I would be exposed to the procedures surrounding hospital admission, I had absolutely no clue that it wouldn't be the last. We were just getting started. By the end of the summer, I would become a pro at all of the hospital procedures.

It all starts with that nifty little hospital bracelet that has your first name, last name and birthday on it. Then comes the part where the nurse (through no fault of their own) must jam an IV into your arm. It's really quite lovely! Moving on. They hand me the same damn robe that I'd sit in for the next five days. The same robe that I'd vomit in. Sweat in. Sleep in.

Those damn robes. I mean, they really are the stupidest garments I have ever seen. You put it on one way and your whole ass is exposed. You put it on the other way and the entire front part of your body is exposed. While I can think of many women who would probably like to sport such an outfit on a Saturday night, I decided to ask the nurse for a second one. It's just common sense. I tie it so that my ass is exposed, and then I tie on the second robe and cover up the backside. It's not a difficult concept, so why didn't she just offer me two to begin with?

Surgery: Round 1

The day after I was admitted into the hospital, I was taken for emergency surgery. They cut me open and took out the cyst. Every move I made was met with gut wrenching pain, and even though I was on painkillers for a few days, I discontinued them almost immediately, not wanting to get addicted to them. I decided to take the pain. It just seemed fitting.

Throughout the night, I would wake up overcome by nausea, and vomited more than on my drunkest night. I'd literally fall asleep in my own vomit. Between the pain, the dizziness, and the never-ending nausea, I didn't care anymore. Nausea. Pain. Sweat. No sleep. Getting into bed hurt, and getting out of bed hurt. Moving hurt.

At night, the nurses would come through and check on all the patients, and I knew which one was coming to check on me based on the sound of their walk and the scent of their perfume. Some of the nurses would walk lightly on their feet, while others would stomp the ground. I was so grateful to hear something other than the moans and groans of the patients from other rooms. I was grateful to hear something other than people sniffling, crying and sobbing; and I was overjoyed to smell their perfume; anything other than that thick smell of a hospital. That *sickly* smell....

When I went home to recover, my entire family never left my side. My mother spent every waking moment asking me if I was okay and if I needed anything. My sister and brother-in-law did the same, ensuring to bring my nephew with them. They knew that nothing would make me smile more than that little boy. While everyone went to work, my grandmother stationed herself by my side and refused to move. She made all of my very favourite dishes, and served them to me like I was some sort of royalty. Sounds like a treat doesn't it? Truth is, she would do the same thing for me with or without surgery. She truly is an amazing person.

After about seven weeks of recovery, I was driving again, going out again, and getting back to normal, finally.

Cancer

I got a phone call to come in for a "follow-up appointment" on the very same day that I got my diagnosis. I went in and was greeted by the same young female doctor. She sat down beside me, very slowly, and had a really cute face that reminded me of someone who would be on a television show. I thought she looked like the actress who played Michelle Dessler on *24*. You know, back when the show was actually good! She was looking at me like her dog just died. She held my hand. I started to shake, anticipating her telling me something terrible, and I told myself to keep it together. There was absolutely nothing I could have done to prepare myself for what I was about to hear.

"I'm sorry Jessica. We ran an autopsy on the cyst that we removed, and we found some cancerous cells. I'm really sorry."

I stared at her for a long time. They say that when you hear really shocking news, denial can kick in. Well, it didn't for me at all. I was shocked, no doubt, but there was no denial. I heard it. I understood it. I had cancer. And I *broke* into a million pieces.

I already told you what my first thought was when I heard this news; but no one ever asked me what my second thought was. My second thought was that I was tired, beyond tired. I was exhausted, and now, I might die at age twenty-nine.

The first tear fell slowly, and the rest quickened. I didn't care anymore who saw me cry and who didn't. I just cried for a really long time. She never let go of my hand. The nurses, the oncologist, and the rest of the staff at the hospital treated me with kindness, patience and sympathy—not pity. Big difference. I detest pity. They made me feel like my case was being treated with all of the attention in the world, and I am so very grateful to them.

My doctor eventually told me it was time for some blood tests, and I walked like a zombie to the neighbouring clinic to get my blood taken. It was time to get pricked with yet another needle, as by now, I'd lost track of how much blood I'd given over that year. It felt like it would have been enough liquid to start my own little lake. I know that I spoke to the nurse as she took out multiple samples of blood, but to this day I have no idea what we talked about.

After that was all over, I realized what the next step would be. I had thought telling my family that I was getting a divorce would be the hardest thing that I would ever have to tell them, but I was wrong. After they watched me go through so much pain just a short time ago, I'd now have to give them more bad news. I looked down at my phone. I had a new text message. It was my sister: "What did the doctor say?"

So now, I had to call my sister and tell her. "How did it go?" she asked. I cried. "What? What happened? Tell me." "They told me I have cancer." There was silence on the phone. For two girls who love to chat, for that moment, there truly was nothing to say. We both cried. After some time, she said something to me that she would repeat throughout this entire ordeal. "Everything will be okay. We'll get through it together. I'm always here with you."

I would soon have to tell my grandmothers, my mother, my brother-in-law, my best friends, my uncles, my aunts and my cousins—that I have cancer. Where the fuck is the instruction book on that?

What's Behind Door #1? Bitter!
What's Behind Door #2? Better!

Another woman had come out of one of the doctors' offices just after I did. She must have been in her mid fifties, and I remembered her from the waiting room. She was in tears. A doctor came to her side and tried to comfort her. "Is there anyone I can call?" she asked. In my own hazy state I can still remember her looking back at the doctor and saying, "No, there's no one."

I spent that evening at my sister's house with her, my brother-in-law, and surrounded by my best friends. I filled them in on everything I had been told. "They said its 'stage one' or something. They said it's called ovarian carcinoma."

I was angry. I was so very angry. Nothing made sense to me. I spent my entire childhood doing "the right thing" taking care of people closest to me, being considerate, practicing kindness, giving to charity, recognizing the needs of others, and helping out wherever and whenever I could. And what was my outcome? I ended up with next to no childhood, the wrong fucking sweater (subject to judgment), and then... cancer. Seriously?

That evening I let anger take over me with no desire or attempt to control it. While everyone who loved me told me that I'd get through this, I paid them no attention. I could feel it in my body. My whole body was on fire, but this time it wasn't because I was carrying a 21cm cyst. This time, my body was reacting to the very angry thoughts that were going through my mind, and I let them run and pulsate through my body with absolutely no effort to stop them. All I could think about was that six hours ago someone told me I had cancer.

A part of my personality kept telling me to calm down, saying, "It's okay Jessica. You'll get through this." But all I could respond with was, "It's NOT OK!" I don't deserve this." And I didn't. But really, who does?

If I continued holding on to the anger that I felt that night, there is no doubt in my mind that I would have ended up opening the wrong door. The anger was just a mask for the fact that I was so incredibly upset for the really shitty hand I had been dealt. I would soon realize the difference between a good and a bad card player. A bad card player looks at his hand, cops out, and folds. A great card player accepts the hand they're dealt, and plays it anyway; and if they're good, I mean really, really good—they win the pot, even though they had the shittiest hand at the table.

Maybe I Do Need a Lucky Rabbit's Foot

On the night of my diagnosis, my anger made a friend. It got really chummy with the whole notion of my "bad luck." I remembered the feeling that snuck into my stomach at that wedding; the same feeling that made me feel like I was that dreadful black cat that crossed someone's path; the feeling that I was "unlucky." And so, I started to buy into it for a little while. *Maybe I really am cursed? How else can I possibly explain the events of my life?*

"You just need some time to have this whole thing sink in," said one of my best friends on the night of my anger spree. Time to sink in? When exactly would that happen?

It was June 26, 2009, and the following week one of my oldest childhood friends was getting married. I was in her bridal party, and we had to meet early for photographs. July 2, 2009 was also the same day of my appointment with my oncologist; the day that I would find out what my next step would be.

Recall: Real

I get bruised. I get broken. I get upset... and then... I *choose* to get better. Now that's real, and I like real.

My emotions were *real* and natural. I mean, who gets told they have cancer and says, "Ohhhh, that's okay. I'm going to think positively now! Wanna go grab a drink?"

But as real of a reaction as it was, it had an expiry date. Being *allowed* to get upset is a reaction that many take for granted. Somehow, they convince themselves that because of their particular struggle, they have every reason to be upset—sometimes, for the rest of their lives.

If you allow those feelings of anger (or any other feelings such as resentment, loneliness, vengeance, or even sadness) to fester, your fate becomes no different than any member of the Stepford Wives Club. So, whether I liked it or not, it was time for me to make a decision.

Decision Time: Bitter or Better?

On the day of my diagnosis, I spent the evening with my sister and my friends, being angry. Perhaps someone had placed some weird Voodoo curse on me? Maybe it was one of those Brownie Bobbitt people? I wouldn't put it past them. Perhaps I should look into some sort of hex removal procedure.

My whole life has been nothing but one gargantuan struggle. When I woke up the next day, I wasn't done being angry, but something else was there too. It was a weird feeling, like my anger had now made another friend. I just couldn't put my hands on what it was, and as much as I focused on how angry I was, I couldn't shake this other feeling. It was like that feeling when you're leaving the house but can't remember if you forgot something, and you just can't stop thinking about it. *What did I forget?* Either way, I decided to pay more attention to the anger.

The next day that same something was still nagging me at the back of my mind, and I still had no clue what it was. *What is it?* It drove me crazy, this thing inside my head, and it bugged me all day. I couldn't place it but felt the anger subsiding, and that in itself was making me angry. I wanted to stay angry, but I couldn't ignore this thing anymore that was creeping up on me. So, reluctantly, I stopped fighting it. I decided to stop drowning out the thoughts that my mind was trying to form, because for the last four days the only part of me that I wanted to acknowledge was the anger. However, this other thing inside my head was just as persistent, and I guess it was time to listen.

For a really long time, I cried, by myself, in my bedroom. The entire time I was crying, I realized why I was crying. Yes, I had cancer and that scared the hell out of me more than words can explain, but I was also crying because I knew that my mountain climb was anything but over. I had really, really hoped that after everything it would *finally* be over, and that maybe I could finally stop climbing. The reason I was crying was because I became increasingly aware of the next battle that I'd have to fight. I was getting into the ring with cancer, and felt like I was wearing some really worn-out gloves. That's when it hit me.

That annoying little voice in my head was getting louder and louder now. It was telling me something, something really important: *In twenty-nine years, I haven't lost one single match. Not one.* When my father needed my support, I provided it. When I lost him at fifteen, I found a way to move on. If I didn't give up at fifteen years of age, why was I willing to give up at twenty-nine? That's ridiculous. It made no sense to me. As a child, I had shown courage, but where was that courage now?

I grew up with a lot of self-esteem issues, but there were always two things about myself that I was proud of: I had never walked away from a responsibility, and my ability to *love* sometimes shocked even me. So, what do I do when this time the responsibility in my life was taking care of *me*? What about when the person who actually needed that love the most this time, was *me*? I was just going to cop out? Give up? Be angry? Now my mind was racing with a hundred and one different thoughts. I didn't get the right sweater for me, but I didn't walk away, and did everything in my power to come up with a "fit" of some sort. When it didn't happen, I picked our happiness over our inevitable demise. I chose to do something that many have only imagined doing, but have never acted on. I chose to do the right thing even though the right thing was the hardest thing to do. And now, I have been diagnosed with cancer.

I have been a lot of things in my life. I've been very sad, I've been confused, and I've lacked confidence in the past; and now I was angry at my fate. Nonetheless, I hadn't given up a day in my life, and there was no way in hell I was about to start now.

I accepted my battle, but I was anything but calm. I was still shocked to have cancer, still very afraid and very sad. What was going to happen to me? The anger was still there, but I was just trying to tell it to shut up.

I wrote it all down, and labelled each day from June 26 to July 1 as "Day 1" to "Day 6." If I got through this cancer bullshit, then that's it. I was gonna finally do it. I was gonna write a book.

July 2 was my friend's wedding, *and* my appointment with the oncologist. My sister refused to allow me to go alone, and came with me to the appointment, staying right by my side.

The oncologist was patient as he sat through our tears, our questions and our fears. He walked us through every potential scenario:

1. The cancer was contained in the cyst, didn't spread, and had already been taken out, but surgery is still needed to investigate further.
2. My ovaries would have to be removed as a precaution, rendering me unable to ever have children. (This thought cut deeper than any of the physical pain I had been in). I'd also go into menopause at age twenty-nine.
3. Chemotherapy and radiation to be administered as a precaution.
4. A hysterectomy. (I don't have any words for this one.)
5. Worse case scenario: the cancer spreads everywhere.

I listened to him explain each and every option, and couldn't believe I was even having this conversation. As he talked, a piece of me *broke* again, and again, and again. I could feel it happening inside of me. He wasn't able to tell me anything for sure, but either way, I was definitely having surgery again. Once he actually did the surgery and could see what was happening inside of me, he would be able to give me more information.

The oncologist did tell me he was optimistic from my test results that I would end up with the first scenario, the best scenario. I had accepted my battle, I had accepted the fact that I needed to be courageous, and I had accepted the fact that I had to let the anger go. But I still didn't have anything to say about the whole "bad luck" thing. I decided that it would be best to prepare myself for the other outcomes.

Use Your Support Systems and Be a Support System

As my sister drove us from the hospital she told me that I didn't have to go to this wedding, and that whatever I wanted to do that day was just fine. I had just gotten a lot of information, and to say it was overwhelming would be an understatement. On top of that, my head was pounding, my eyes were heavy, and my brain was fried. I decided to just go home. I needed time to process everything. But before I could open my mouth to say it, all I could think of was *hypocrite*.

The thoughts of a couple of days ago crept back up on me in that car ride home. I reminded myself of one of the things that I have always prided myself on most: my ability to love. And there I was, about to tell my sister to take me home, to take me home when one of my childhood friends was getting married. I wasn't going to miss my friend's wedding. At that very moment I realized that no matter what direction my doctor would take, I was going to lose more time in surgery, in recovery, in limbo; and the thought of missing out on anything else made me very uncomfortable. Yes, a huge part of me wanted to go home, get under the covers of my bed and stay there. But it just didn't feel right.

My sister raced home and helped me throw on

my sari—literally! I got to the banquet hall and felt like I was in the *Twilight Zone*. An hour and a half ago I was in my oncologist's office discussing how to proceed with my cancer, and now I was walking into a wedding, smiling and hugging all of my friends, aunts and uncles, and getting my photo taken. Say cheese!

As I watched my two friends exchange their vows, I was unable to forget about the cancer inside of my body. I was unable to forget the fact that there may be a possibility I would never be able to have children. There are no words to explain the fear I was experiencing about what would happen to me, but I knew I didn't have any control over this. I just had to let life happen, and life was going to happen with or without me. This wedding was going to happen, with or without me, so while I still had the choice, I *chose* to be a part of it.

Today wasn't about me, it was about them; and I'm happy to have shared in it with them.

The next day at the wedding reception, my family silently supported me from across the room with a smile or a nod, just to remind me that they were there with me.

I decided it was time to party. I got pretty drunk. It was fantastic.

The Bitter & Better "Waiting Room"

On August 17, 2009, I would get to wear those infamous hospital gowns all over again. I was haunted by thoughts of nausea, vomiting, pain, being unable to move, and the endless nights thinking about the success of my surgery. Would it work? Had the cancer spread? Would I be able to have children? Would I have to go through chemo?

The last three thoughts haunted me more than anything else. I couldn't sleep in the weeks leading up to the surgery. All I could think about was if at that very moment, cancer was spreading in different areas of my body. If so, where was it moving to, and what does that mean? Would I survive it? These thoughts were so terrifying that it would cause my body to start shaking.

My mind would drift to something very precious to me: children. I thought of not being able to have them, and how cruel it was to take away the ability for a woman to have children. I may never be able to bring a part of me into this world. I've never been opposed to adoption, but I'd never imagined the choice to have my own would be taken away from me. I felt robbed at the thought of how people always say, "Oh, he has your eyes," or, "She has your smile," and I thought about the possibility of going through life and never hearing those words.

In my mind, I saw myself losing my hair, vomiting, and crying. The thought was so frightening that I'd instantly try and think of something else to make the image go away as fast as possible.

Before my next surgery, I had to go into the hospital for some "pre-surgery work." This is when they take some blood, ask you some questions, take your height and weight, go through your medications, and so on. Just like any hospital, you have to wait your turn, and

I sat there with a magazine. I really didn't know why I bothered, seeing as I would just end up re-reading the same sentence over and over again. My nerves were shot, and the same terrifying thoughts were still haunting me. *Had the cancer spread? Would I be able to have children?* Sometimes, just looking at a child's face would be enough to make my heart sink.

Adamant about keeping my mind off these thoughts, I scanned the room. I had been coming to this office for a while now, so some faces were becoming familiar to me. The women in the waiting room were in their fifties and sixties; and then of course, there was me. Most of them were in the midst of treatment and walked in with a hat or a bandana tied around their head. Some walked in looking pale, weak and fragile. They had all evidently been through hell.

There were two dominant groups of women. The first group were patients of the same doctor, and sat in silence for the most part. When they did speak, I found myself very uncomfortable in their presence as they complained about waiting times, the hospital, and the staff. They all seemed to have a complaint about their kid, their ex, their daughter-in-law, etc. There was a lot of sighing, and it was really rather annoying. Could I blame them for being in a bad mood? No, I guess I couldn't; especially after the hell they had been through. I just couldn't tell if it was a temporary thing or if they were always like this. I instantly felt a sense of déjà vu, and remembered the first time I ever met the Brown Stepford Wives clubs. I recalled the promise I had made to myself back then; that I would never walk down that bitter path.

The other group of women were undergoing aggressive treatments. They looked exhausted and in pain, but there was something different about them. They chatted. Not much, but they chatted, and asked each other how they were feeling. They swapped tips on how to fall asleep at night, how to combat nausea, how to explain to their kids and their families that they would be okay and not to worry. I felt a little guilty for eavesdropping, but I couldn't help it. They were unbelievable, and I was in awe of them.

It felt like the hospital waiting room was a purgatory for the bitter club or the better club. It didn't take much for me to decide which group I'd rather belong to.

One woman noticed me, smiled, and asked me if I was waiting for someone. I couldn't help it. I burst into laughter. She looked really surprised by my reaction. I said, "Nope, I'm here because I was told I have ovarian cancer and I have to go for surgery." I could tell she was surprised. All you had to do was take one look around the room to see how odd I looked in the midst of much older women. I could tell she wanted to know how old I was. "I'm twenty-nine," I said.

We get to chatting and she explained that she'd been there for a few hours. She had just had a chemo treatment and couldn't go home yet. I learned that her husband had passed away many years ago, and she has two children, a daughter and a son. They don't come with her to her chemo treatments. They don't come to see her at her home. They're "busy," and so she took public transit here and will take a cab back. She could only afford a cab one way.

"You don't seem angry with them," I said. "I was. I really was," she responded, "but my only priority is beating this thing, with or without their help." She didn't sound the least bit angry, just ready to beat it. She told me about a really great organization called Ovarian Cancer Canada, where she does volunteer work as she undergoes chemotherapy. I was in awe of her, and could see that she was scared, but strong too. I smiled at her and reassured her that she would beat it. We both will. And we both did.

As my mind floated back to the day of my diagnosis, I remembered the woman who told the doctor that there was "no one to call." I looked at my new friend before me and wished that her kids would call her. Just once.

From a really young age, I became used to managing my own feelings. When it came to ordeals such as my divorce and my cancer, I did just that: I tried to sort out what I was feeling on my own. Spending some time on your own and reflecting about what you're feeling and how you want to move forward is very important, but it's only half the battle. Venting with the people that I loved most made me feel supported, loved and cared for. The trick is finding the best listeners.

Every time I needed to rely on that help and support from my family and friends, they were there. I am grateful to them, all of them, for always loving me. From that day onward, I couldn't shake these other women from my mind; the same women who were still battling out some struggle or another, with no one to call. I thought of them all the time.

Five Requests

My pre-surgery dinner was cherry popsicles: a standard pre-surgery meal. My mom slept beside me that night, and I knew how badly she wanted to make this all go away for me. She would have given anything to see it all just disappear, and I could see it all over her face.

I lay in bed imagining what would happen to me tomorrow. Would he cut me open and then tell me I could never have children? Would he tell me that the cancer had spread to areas that he just didn't anticipate? Or would he tell me everything was okay? It was a never-ending circle of worry and sadness that made my heart ache.

I prayed that night. I knew that the next day my fate and my life may change in so many different ways based on what this disease could do to my body. I prayed for good health and the hope that the cancer was contained. I prayed for the ability to have children. And then, I said this:

> Whatever happens to me, I pray for five things—the same five things that I saw in my new friend from the waiting room: Strength, love, character and integrity,

generosity, and forgiveness. I asked for strength to continue to climb this mountain until I reached the top; and love to keep my heart warm and far from anger, far from *bitter*. I asked to be a person of integrity; to remain generous to the people and causes around me; that I be forgiven for all of my own mistakes and to learn how to forgive all of the people who have ever really hurt me, regardless of if they had ever actually apologized or not.

I didn't sleep for one second that night. It dawned on me that I had made the choice to get *better* before the surgery had even taken place. I decided that before the doctor even had a chance to operate, I had chosen *better*, and would accept whatever fate that was coming my way with the knowledge that no matter what happened, I would find my way.

It was the weirdest feeling I have ever had. On one hand, I was so very proud of myself for making that choice, and on the other hand, I was still shaking with more fear than I have ever felt in my entire life.

Surgery: Round 2

I woke up in the morning with my heart beating out of my chest, and got to the hospital in disbelief that I was going for another surgery. *This is it*, I thought as I checked in through registration.

I got my bracelet and my robes. My eyes were stinging. Here we go. Lying on the operating table, the oncologist asked me to count from ten to one. I think I got to four, and then I woke up in the recovery area with a familiar sense of nausea and pain. After the surgery, the oncologist told my family everything had gone well, but after some further testing he would know for sure what our next steps would be.

I went home for recovery with my mind dancing in the same torturous questions: *Children, chemo, cancer spreading, adoption, freezing eggs, radiation, sperm donors, I must get pregnant immediately, losing parts of my body… death; back to children, back to chemo*. Again and again and again.

Lucky #21

I went back to the oncologist to find out what he had learned from the test results.

"Do I want to know?" I said.

"It looks like I was right," he began. "The cancer was contained in the removed cyst, and from what we can see, has not spread anywhere else."

"What?"

He smiled, "Great news isn't it?"

"Yes… that's it?"

"That's it."

"No chemo?"

"Nope."

"No radiation?"

"Nope. Just regular check-ups with me every three months."

He shook my hand.

"Why did this happen? I got a 21cm cyst. What if it comes back?"

"The cyst you got was very rare."

"Ya, the first doctor the first time around told me I was 'one in a million.'"

"Perhaps you are."

"Gee, thanks. Just a stroke of bad luck I guess!"

"Bad luck or good luck. All in your interpretation."

I looked at him like he was a lunatic.

"Jessica, I wish more women would come screaming into the hospital in pain because they had a 21cm cyst. Ovarian cancer is called the "silent killer" for a reason. I wish more women who are victims to ovarian cancer got the same red flags that you did so that we *know* something is wrong, and we can treat them. Unfortunately, most women are diagnosed in the latter stages once the cancer has already spread. Your cancer contained itself in a cyst and then forced you, in pain, to come to the hospital so that we could get it treated. Your body warned you that something was wrong so that we could fix you. None of this is typical of ovarian cancer."

"Oh," I said.

"Sounds damn lucky to me," he concluded.

Thank Your Lucky Scars

Before my second surgery, I was told I'd be left with five scars that would be very faint, resembling slight pencil marks on my stomach. I saw someone else's scars who went through a similar surgery, and that's exactly what they looked like. In fact, you could hardly see them unless you stared really closely.

When I took the bandages off my stomach, what I saw beneath those bandages did not resemble pencil marks. They looked more like thick lines drawn in by a permanent marker. Unknown to me at the time, my body is prone to keloids—scars that don't heal in the same way as other peoples' scars do. My doctor told me that there really is no rhyme or reason for that. It's just the way your body heals. In addition, I was only supposed to have five scars, but instead, I had six! Apparently, they were going to laser one area of my body (the entrance point to where they would be operating), but it didn't work out, and they had to go to another spot; so I ended up with a sixth scar.

I couldn't believe what I was seeing in the mirror, and my first reaction was sadness. I didn't know how I'd ever wear a bathing suit again, or even a sari for that matter. I've since caught women staring at my scars in the locker room at the gym. Then they notice me noticing them, and very quickly look away, embarrassed. Five of the six scars are small but thick, and the one right in the middle of my stomach is the largest, and the thickest. They're not massive, but they're obvious, and I guess people were curious as to what they were. Maybe I can't blame them for that, and as much as I didn't like them either, I told myself, quite frankly, to shut up. I had been given an incredible blessing. Things could have worked out very differently.

I spent the next few months taking it easy,

recovering from surgery, catching up at work, spending time with my friends and family, and saying thank you every single day for the outcome that I was blessed with. Now that I had a lot of my strength back, it was time to make good on my word. It was time to start my book. I pulled out all of the notes I had made while I was going through my cancer ordeal; went through them, and that's when I saw the five things I had prayed for: Strength, love, character and integrity, generosity, and forgiveness.

    I guess the saying, "Be careful what you wish for," is true. I wished for five wonderful things, and was given five strong and courageous reminders on my abdomen to reflect on the person I had promised to be—with one extra scar for good luck.

Better Better Better!

One of my best friends works for the Ontario Medical Association. They were reaching out to their employees and asking for "touching and unique stories" that would help in their Ontario's Doctors campaign.

    I'm nothing if not unique. My friend shared my story with them, and they contacted me to ask if I'd be willing to participate in their campaign. A girl who is notoriously known for being private was now being asked to pose for a billboard that would later be displayed in the heart of downtown Toronto. I agreed.

    A picture of me, with my hair tied up in a ponytail,

was being displayed in subway shelters, buses, magazines, and a huge billboard that read:

> "When I was 29, doctors discovered I had a large cyst—it was cancerous. I was terrified, but my oncologist understood what was happening to me, and he helped me understand it too. Now I'm cancer-free, and I can't thank him enough, not just for treating me, but also for never letting me lose hope."

At the bottom it said: "Jessica's Life is Our Life's Work. Ontario Medical Association."

When I saw the image for the first time, I was tempted to ask the photographer to perhaps work some Photoshop magic on my face. It was close after the surgery, and I had put on some weight after sitting on my butt for so long during recovery. I thought about it for a while and realized that if I Photoshop my face, then I have no right to talk about being "real." I decided to leave it.

If there was even one young woman out there who saw my poster and realized that she wasn't the only one going through this at such a young age, then it was all worth it. If it showed women of all ages that recovery was possible, if I was able to instill hope in even one woman, I'd have posed for that picture a thousand times over.

At the beginning I was hesitant to have my face plastered all over downtown Toronto, but my friends loved the idea, including the receptionist at my oncologist's waiting room. "You should definitely do this," she encouraged. "I bet your message will bring all kinds of good luck to other women who have been diagnosed with ovarian cancer." It took a moment for what she said to sink in. This random stranger just told me that I'd bring "good luck" to others. Right then I was reminded of the woman who didn't want me to touch the bride and groom's "life tying knot." I chuckled to myself. Things really do have a way of coming full circle.

Today

It still happens sometimes. I still hear the whispers around me from various *bitter* clubs: "Geez, can't this girl catch a break?" or, "That poor girl." Of course my personal favourite is the gush of whispers released into the air whenever I walk into a room. "Yup, that's her!" says one gossip to the other. (Someone really needs to tell these people that they're *not* whispering... I can hear you!) Then, they'd just sit there staring at me with what I think was *supposed* to be a smile on their face, but was usually about as genuine as Paris Hilton at a charity fundraiser. The funny thing is, those whispers, then and now, have always been the least damaging to my ego. What actually hurt me the most, and always made me feel like I got a raw deal, were the whispers in my own head. The *decent* people around me were never "whispering" at all. They just wanted to see me happy and healthy. (Notice the emphasis on "decent.")

Today, I'm more than just happy and healthy. I am very proud of who I am, and there isn't a day that goes by that I don't stop to look at myself (and my lucky scars) in the mirror and say, "Damn! Good for you! Keep moving! Never stop."

And I never will.

Through the help of the extraordinary medical system in Ontario, I am doing great today. It seems that people I know (and even people I don't) like to congratulate me and tell me how "strong" and "resilient" they think I am. At one time, those "compliments" made me feel awkward, but now I understand why they made me feel that way. Those words made me feel different, and were a constant reminder that I didn't seem to fit into the norm. I've felt different my whole life because I faced unique challenges at ages when most kids were jumping rope or playing baseball. But I was bored of being "different," and just wanted to be like everyone else. I wanted to fit into that standard norm. Not anymore.

I'm perfectly fine with being one in a million.

Regular Check-Ups

When I go for my regular check-ups at the hospital, even though the oncologist is the same and the hospital is the same, everything else is very different. Regardless of what area in the hospital I walk to, I no longer smell *it* anymore. It doesn't smell like "sick people" anymore. Whenever I go back to that very same hospital, it feels like I'm in a wonderful place surrounded by amazing people who are all working their asses off to make the best out of a whole bunch of really tough situations. I feel so very grateful to be living in a country where I have received such phenomenal care, and it's something that I remember daily.

The admission procedure is still the same. I go in and provide two types of health card while I wait for my name to be called. Once I get called, the first thing I do is get ready for my ultrasound, where the nurse hands me two robes (smart lady she is, I didn't even have to tell her I needed two). I'm being checked, I'm being monitored, and again—I'm damn grateful for that.

I remember the first ultrasound I went to after my surgery (I've had dozens since then). The technician uses liquid to make your stomach all slippery so that they can take a look inside of you. Then comes the *fun* part where they take a rather large prong and inject it inside of you, and poke… and prod… and take pictures. The entire time she's doing that I'm scanning her face, trying to read her expression as she looks at the images on the screen. *Does she see anything? Is something there? Is something wrong?* She won't tell me though, even if I ask. She's not allowed to. When it's all over, I sit on the edge of the bed and wait while the pictures are sent to a radiologist, wondering if the radiologist is going to come and talk to me. *Why are they making me wait here so long? Did my old cyst leave behind an evil twin sister? They would only make me wait if they saw something terrible, right? Maybe I have cancer all over again.*

At this point, I remember my decision to choose *better*. I will not allow my mind to go this way because once I do, it'll lead me to a whole bunch of other thoughts that slowly fester, take over, and become very, very *bitter*. That's not who I am, and I will never allow that to happen.

I'm grateful that the technician always chats with me about what I did on the weekend to try and help me occupy my thoughts. I let them do their job while I do mine—to focus on the five things I promised I would practice no matter what happens tomorrow: Strength, love, character and integrity, generosity, and forgiveness.

My Own Personal Prozac

I am thankful that I found my love for writing, reading and music. They act as my medicine, they make me smile, they make me happy, and they remind me to be *better*.

I thank three generations of women for always loving me: a grandmother who is the very epitome of love and selflessness in every move she makes, a mother who reminds me of how much she loves me in just the way she looks at me, and a sister who adamantly refused to leave my side no matter what new hurdle came my way. I am convinced that their love for me, and my unconditional love for them, will always work better than any pill any doctor could ever prescribe. Love from those around you will always work better than Prozac. Never ever forget to rely on your support systems. More importantly, never ever forget to be a support system. Never forget to *give back*.

Is "life is busy" a truism? Yes. Is it a bit of a cop out? Yes.

By no means am I suggesting that we must all sign ourselves up for every last charity within a fifty mile radius, engage in fundraisers every weekend, and make it our life's mission to save every endangered species. What I am suggesting is that we give back.

Before you go out and try and save the entire world, you may just want to start closer to home. From a very young age I learned that the more I ever lent a helping hand financially or emotionally, the more my financial and emotional bank account grew to a very modest yet decent standard of living. When you loosen the grip on what's "mine" and what's "yours," the outcome is really amazing. You begin to see more of what's "ours." I suggest you try it some time. That's the thing, karma can be a bitch, and it can also be your best friend.

Remember the people who love you: the people who have always loved you. Remember the people that would give you the last dollar in their wallet, no questions asked. Remember the people that have never left your side, and ask yourself: Have I given back? Have I *truly* given back?

My commitment to my family had been life long, but I still felt a void; and so I decided to make a commitment to two organizations that were very close to my heart. Ovarian Cancer Canada is an organization with a mission to overcome ovarian cancer by providing support, awareness, and funding to the cause. When I've been able to make the time, I have taken part in their Listen to the Whispers program: An initiative where volunteers speak publicly of the very "silent symptoms" of ovarian cancer in efforts to spread awareness of this "silent killer." I wish someone had heard of my symptoms and had been able to guide me. The most I ever heard after explaining my severe bloating and lower back pain was, "Wow, that's really bizarre."

If anything I say in any of those meetings drives a woman to the doctor to get diagnosed as soon as possible, I will gladly take part as much as I possibly can.

I am also a part of a charitable organization called everyday child (www.everydaychild.org). Once I heard the central aims of this organization, I knew immediately that I wanted to be a part of it:

Every child has the right to live.
Every child has the right to be loved.
Every child has the right to laugh.
Every child has the right to dream.
Every child has the right to a future.

The mission of this organization is to encourage leadership and foster skills and talents among individuals by engaging them in activities guided by an underlying principle: Learn, Earn, Return. Our target audience is the entire world. By reaching out to the slums in Mumbai as a starting point, our goals are to create an environment where kids can truly be kids. They can learn, they can play, and they can dream. I sit in meetings with my fellow colleagues, and excitement and happiness bursts through my body. They all feel the same sense of passion as I do toward the same cause.

I don't necessarily think I had the opportunity to be an everyday child; not in its entirety. I definitely had a lot to be grateful for: a roof over my head, family that loved and cared about me, and the privilege of going to school. But no matter what, my mind was usually focused on fulfilling a responsibility, being there for those who needed me, and lending a helping hand. I don't regret that for one second.

The reality is that I didn't pursue my loves and talents at a time when they were just being born. However, there's no time like the present!

I think of the everyday children in our world who possess all kinds of talents and skills, and no one knows about them. In slums and poverty-filled areas we could potentially stumble upon the next Van Gogh or Martin Luther King. I know that I want to find them. We have the ability to foster the skills of a young and budding piano player, photographer or sculptor. I know they're out there, and through this remarkable organization, I want to help find them and further their aspirations.

I can't fully describe the feeling of providing a child (who works longer hours than any of us in the developed world) an opportunity to play and to engage in creative arts, to learn about photography, and to run around and get dirty. It feels damn good, and maybe that's why I went through what I went through. Maybe I was destined to do this. Maybe I wasn't. I don't know, and I no longer care about the "whys" either way.

I'm doin' it, and I *love* it.

The View From Up Top

I had been broken: again and again, and again. I never wanted to be the person who refused to take off the sweater because I was scared to get *broken*. Getting broken *repeatedly* was the best thing that has ever happened to me. It can be the best thing that has ever happened to you too, if you let it. It builds character. It builds strength. It builds love, and it makes you a stronger, faster and *better* mountain climber.

I hope that you'll take some time in your life to identify when you were bruised, when you broke, and then what you decided to do about it. Did you allow yourself the opportunity to have a *real* reaction? Did you vent it out? Are you still venting it out? Still angry? Sad? Are you moving on?

When the choice presented itself to you, did you *choose bitter* or *better*? And if you made the wrong choice back then, just know that you absolutely can change it now.

If you *want* to.

I guess that leaves only one final question? When the hell can we stop climbing that mountain?

Never.

You never stop climbing that mountain. In fact, I no longer want to stop climbing that mountain. The day we stop climbing is the day we give up. It's the day we no longer have anything to climb for.

As far as getting to the top—I made a mistake on that one. I didn't realize it right away, but I've gotten there already, numerous times. I climbed my way to the top when I was seven years old; again when I was fifteen; and again and again throughout my teen years. I climbed my way to the top after I got divorced, and again when I got diagnosed with cancer. Now, I think I'm gonna take in the view for a bit. Everything looks amazing when you're sitting on top of the world.

I'm ready though, for my next climb; and I'm sure it will be *better* than the last.

Did I Just Do That?

A colleague at work told me that I am the last person she ever expected to speak of their personal life in a book. I would have to agree with her. No, I didn't divulge every last detail of my life, but I'd say that this is a pretty decent chunk. So what makes someone known for being so private write so openly? Three things drove me to do this.

One. I've relied on my support system, and I am a support system. I've met a lot of people who don't have the magnificent support system that many of us have do, and I write this book in an effort to reach out to those people.

I have definitely climbed my share of mountains, but I didn't always climb them alone. I've been surrounded by a wonderful family and by people who take the meaning of friendship very seriously. I was never put in a position where I had to tell my doctor that there was "no one to call".

I genuinely enjoy making people feel better, and I absolutely detest seeing people upset. Call it corny if you like, but I literally feel awful inside when I see someone else in pain, struggling, or feeling alone. For whatever reason, when I have provided guidance and support to another human being, I end up feeling like a million bucks. Maybe that makes me selfish in my own right. I know that I don't have the power to cure everyone of their heartaches, but I see absolutely nothing wrong in trying. Through my writing, I hope to reach as wide an audience as possible to do just that. I've learned that I want to make people feel better whenever and wherever I can.

Two. Happy, sad, in love, heartbroken, content, or just getting by: I ask you to challenge your own thinking. Perhaps something you read here might just get you to move in a direction that never existed on your mental compass before.

Three. On July 1, 2009, I promised myself that if I was healthy, I would write a book—and here it is. The strength of someone's word is gold. It isn't always, but it always should be.

Mountain Climbing

Your Mission:

You have now successfully completed part one of your mission. I am very proud of you, and you're not far from victory now.

It's time to tackle part two.

PART 2:
The Bitter Battlefield

Life Principles to Take with You in Battle

I promised that I wouldn't send you out in such a dangerous battlefield without providing you with the necessary tools for victory.

RSVP

We all get the invitation, and if you haven't gotten it yet, just know that you will. Maybe not today, and maybe not tomorrow, but I guarantee you that it will come when you least expect it (or maybe even when you most expect it), there it will be, waiting for you to RSVP. Some of you have already received it and have sent back your reply. Some of you checked off the right box, and some of you checked off the wrong box. The oddest thing about this particular invitation card is that you can change your RSVP at any time. This can be a terrible or a fantastic thing.

The invitation card looks something like this:

INVITATION TO: Your name here
EVENT: The Bruised, Broken 'n' Bitter Club!
DATE: For the rest of your life
TIME: Starting now!

☐ Yes, I will attend
☐ No, I will not attend

The Bitter Battlefield

Be honest with yourself. Which box did you check off?

I can no longer keep track of how many times throughout my life I have been invited to this club. Whether it was the Brown Stepford Wives Club, The Stepford Wannabees, the Bobbit Brownies, or my ordeal with cancer, I saw that the members of the Bruised, Broken 'n' Bitter Club didn't waste any time. The very second a member of this club learned I was dealing with trying times, they wanted me to join. Just like any other club, the more members they could recruit, the larger they would grow. The larger they got, the more powerful they became; and the more influence they acquired, the more their message would be heard.

I should warn you now. The sales people on this team are one of the best I have ever seen. They deliver what appears to be convincing arguments to sign up for membership, or at the very least, attend one of their meetings. They appear to be resourceful, experienced, and sometimes even wise. I've heard the pitch numerous times, and I can confidently say that some of these sales people have the capability of selling lemons to a lemonade stand.

Would you join a gym without taking a tour of the facility? Would you accept a job with a company without researching what they're all about first? Would you volunteer your time with a charity if you didn't believe in their cause? I didn't think so. So before you can decide if you want to be a member of this club, I suggest you attend a meeting.

Their meetings are open to everyone and anyone; and where do you think the bitter clubs meet? Some sort of dive? A dingy, tiny room with floors that creak? Wrong. They hold their meetings at 5-star hotels and restaurants, in conference rooms bigger than my backyard, and they have caviar, wine and champagne. It truly is amazing: the illusion of how wonderful something can look at first glance.

The first time one of the bitter clubs ever invited me to join, I ran faster than I've ever run in my life. I wondered how many other people out there were curious enough to attend a meeting. How many of these people went back for a second or third meeting, or subscribed to a lifetime membership? How many members did they now have? I shudder at the thought.

I definitely knew I didn't want to join, but in good conscience, I couldn't just stand by and watch while others became members. The club would prey on people who lacked support systems and who were dealing with struggle after struggle. I couldn't just allow this group to grow bigger and more powerful, and so I did something. I joined the competition. I hope to see you there.

The Competitive Market

Coke has Pepsi. McDonalds has Burger King. Women have other women.

Everyone has a competitor, and The Bruised Broken 'n' Bitter Club is no different. Just like them, their major competitor also meets regularly and will send you an invitation card regularly throughout your life.

The invitation card looks something like this:

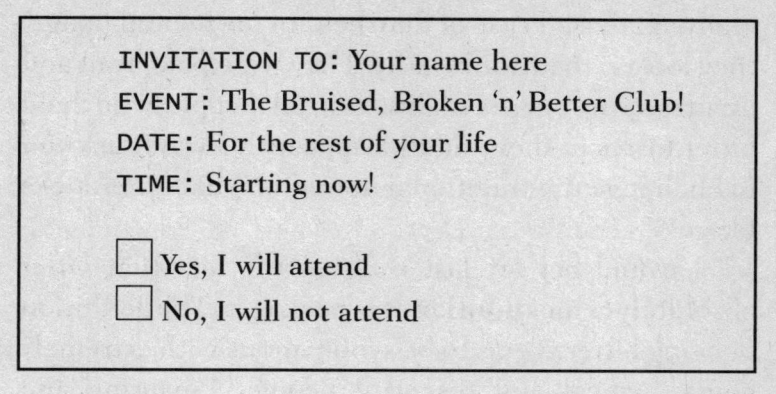

INVITATION TO: Your name here
EVENT: The Bruised, Broken 'n' Better Club!
DATE: For the rest of your life
TIME: Starting now!

☐ Yes, I will attend
☐ No, I will not attend

It's odd, the amount of people who claim that their invitation to this particular club got lost in the mail.

Accept this invitation and I promise you will win on the battlefield. Otherwise, it's like trying to fire a gun with no bullets. Your ammunition is to fall in love.

What does it mean to fall in love? Falling in love is anything that makes your heart ecstatic! For me, it was my love for writing, music, and my family and friends. Whatever it is: Find it! Practice it! Love it!

Fall in love once a day—at the bare minimum!

Be Wary of Bitter: It Can Disguise Itself

Picture what *bitter* looks like in your mind. Don't over think it, just close your eyes and see what your brain comes up with. Go ahead, close your eyes.

I did the very same exercise and conjured up an image of a human being with a sour look on their face. They sat and walked with terrible posture, had nothing nice to say, and were about as comforting as a really, really bad case of diarrhea. In my mental image, they looked really unhealthy. They were pale, frail and unattractive; but in reality, not all people who hold bitter tastes in their mouths appear this way. I ask you to challenge the traditional notion of what *bitter* looks like.

I would bet my last Rolo on the fact that *bitter* absolutely comes in all kinds of packages. The definition of being bitter seems to be synonymous with extremely angry, cynical and resentful people. Lingering and extreme feelings of sadness, loneliness, selfishness, feeling taken for granted, feeling unappreciated, and an overall unhappiness are all a part of being bitter too. These feelings cause human beings to lash out, to isolate themselves, to repress feelings, and to act in a variety of ways that perhaps they normally would not.

In simplest terms, when these feelings fester, your mind and body will react.

Getting Better: Your Health

We all have massive energy running through our bodies every single day, and how we choose to exert and channel that energy will decide the fate of our health: physically and mentally.

When we're running to catch the bus, streetcar or subway to get to work, to make it to that 8 a.m. meeting on a Monday morning that some fool scheduled; we're using that energy.

When we're in a heated argument with a loved one; we're using that energy. When we're thinking about something that bothers us, makes us feel badly, or even devastates us, and we replay it over and over again in our minds; we're using that energy.

When we're plowing away at a passion that we love, and that meal, that canvas, or our garden is finally coming to life; we're using that energy too!

I want to share with you, really share with you, the extent in which your mental health and physical health are interrelated. There is nothing independent about your mind or your body—they are spectacularly interconnected.

Your thought process, your day-to-day mindset, the people and the energy you choose to surround yourself with, your emotions, your innermost feelings, the food and drink that you choose to consume, your level of happiness, your level of sorrow, your aspirations, your lack of aspirations, your passions, your lack of passion, and of course, *choosing* to make your heart ecstatic or miserable—this will decide the fate of your mental and physical health.

Permanent anger can lead to high blood pressure, headaches, stomachaches, and a weaker immune system; and this is just the beginning my friends.

According to a research study conducted by a group of Norwegian and English researchers, and published in the British Journal of Psychiatry, depression is just as bad for you as smoking. It was found that both groups of people share something in common. They both tend to engage in little physical activity; which as we all know is a contributing factor to acquiring heart disease.

The BBC reports findings from a variety of studies that indicate how higher levels of depression more than double your chances of acquiring Alzheimer's disease.

Hostility is also bad for your health. The UC Berkeley Wellness Letter, an authoritative online health newsletter, summarized multiple studies that found how hostility can increase the risk of heart attack. Their report states that approximately 40 percent of people admitted feeling angry or quite upset within two hours of suffering a stroke.

Loneliness is also detrimental to your health. Two psychologists from the University of Chicago examined the toll that loneliness takes on physical well-being. The findings of this study are published by the Arthritis Foundation and explain that the effects of loneliness may be minimal when a person is younger, but physical breakdown due to feelings of loneliness will increase over time. What really amazed me were the differences in urine samples from self-confessed lonely people, and those who felt content. Lonely people had higher levels of Epinephrine in their body. We have often heard of this as the body's "fight or flight" response to intense situations. The higher the levels of Epinephrine, the higher the risk of physical breakdown as you age; although the younger, lonely generation are not quite in the clear. This study also examined the sleep patterns of young content individuals and compared them to those who were young and lonely. It was found that those who experienced loneliness suffered from "micro awakenings" in their sleep. In simplest terms, they had poorer sleep quality then their content counterparts.

Dr. John Cacioppo, founder and director of the University of Chicago Centre for Cognitive and Social Neuroscience, explains that loneliness will have a *major* impact on our physical and mental health. Using resources such as brain scans, he examined the effects of social interactions on our health, and claims that, "Loneliness lowers the ability to control yourself. It is really easy after a bad day to have a second scotch and a third to get some comfort."

We've all heard the expression "dying from a broken heart" Is it just an expression? Not according to findings published in the British Medical Journal, which reported that men had a 40 percent higher risk of dying within six months of losing their spouse.

Not yet convinced on the loneliness argument? One of the most interesting studies I found is called the "conjugal condition," conducted by a British epidemiologist called William Farr in 1858. Now I know what you're thinking: times have definitely changed since 1858? Well, kind of. Stay with me on this one. Farr's objective was to study the effect that marriage had on a person's health. He divided the adult population into three distinct categories: Those who are married, those who have never married or where celibate, and the widowed. It was found that those who were unmarried died from disease in exceptionally higher levels than those who were married. It also showed that those who were widowed had the highest levels of poor health out of all three groups.

This study is obviously outdated as it's a new world and not everyone decides to get married anymore. Some people engage in common law relationships and live their lives the same way as married people do. And what about gay couples? This study didn't account for them at all? The point is that Farr was definitely on the right path. His discovery may not account for today's society, but contemporary studies that take cohabitation into account have come up with the same results. For example, researchers in Sweden found that those who cohabitate or are married at midlife have a lower risk of acquiring any form of dementia. It seems that in the century since Farr's work, the advantage of the marriage debate has gotten stronger, and for good reason. In the Netherlands, researchers studied the causes of two dozen deaths, and in almost every category, the unmarried were always at a prior emotional or physical health disadvantage. Homicide and cancer were examples of the categories studied. Other contemporary research has shown that married people are less likely to acquire pneumonia, undergo surgery, develop cancer, or suffer from a heart attack.

What about those who are married and unhappy? Remember the goal here is to be happy and married... not just married. One is merely a title, the other a reality. Troubled relationships can leave a person far less healthy than if they had never married at all.

Farr's work pointed contemporary social scientists

in the right direction, even though he definitely exaggerated the institution of marriage and underplayed the value of the actual relationship. It's not enough to just be married. A healthy and happy relationship itself is crucial for a happy and healthy life.

Optimism! What a powerful word with a powerful impact. What is it that makes optimism so good for your health? According to Harvard Health Publications, a part of the explanation is behavioural. It seems that the major differences between optimists and pessimists is that optimists tend to engage in healthier lifestyle practices, have close-knit relationships, and are less likely to smoke and more likely to exercise.

Over eight hundred people were evaluated on a psychological test that measured their levels of optimism and pessimism in addition to a medical evaluation. For every ten-point increase in pessimism within the psychological test, the mortality rate rose by 19 percent.

A University of London study examined ten thousand individuals from Britain and questioned them on their wealth, health and social ties. It seems that the satisfaction derived from social interactions is equivalent to earning more money annually. The Journal of Socio-Economics features the findings of Dr. Nattavudh Powdthavee, assistant professor of economics, showing that "an improvement in health from very poor to excellent provides as much happiness as an extra $631,000 a year." Conversely, excellent to poor health has a mental effect on an individual equivalent to losing $480,000. It also shows that being a widow has a mental affect similar to a loss of $421,000 in the same year, and getting hitched reportedly provides a gain equivalent to $105,000 for that year. According to this investigation, almost all of us have what Professor Daniel Gilbert from Harvard University calls "affective forecasting": the sense that we fail to predict what would make us happier in the future.

A 2008 analysis conducted by researchers from Harvard Medical School and the University of California, San Diego, examined approximately five thousand individuals over twenty years. They found that happiness can spread through social networks like an "emotional contagion." Apparently, when one person is happy, that happiness disperses to a network of three. One person's happiness triggers a chain reaction that benefits his friends, his friends' friends, and so on, rippling outwards for up to a year.

Remember that expression: "Laugh and the whole world laughs with you. Cry, and you cry alone". The researchers used a metric for studying depression called the Center for Epidemiological Studies Depression Index. The conclusion was that, "Conversely, sadness does not spread thorough social networks as robustly as happiness."

Be mindful that your mind and your body are loyal to one another. They are the best of friends. If you upset one, the other is definitely going to have something to say about it.

Healing and Forgiveness: Find Your Magic Wand

I wish I had a magic wand to perform mind-boggling miracles. All I would have to do is wave it around in my hand and ask for something using the words "please" and "thank you," and *tad-a*: there it would be. Along with asking to meet Jay-Z and Beyoncé (and trying to convince them to allow me to write songs for them), and a chit chat with Tina Fey (one of the best writers of all time)—I would ask for the capability of curing every single person in the world of their heartache. I wish it was just that easy. I wish that we all had a magic wand of our own and that every single time someone felt grief, felt sorrow, felt resentment, felt alone, felt an emotional pain so deep that it took away their desire to eat and their capability to sleep—all I would have to do is wave that magic wand and, *voilà*: they felt magnificent! I would give anything to have that capability.

We all experience emotional pain in our own ways, and we all move on from it differently. Unfortunately, life and love do not come with instruction manuals. We have to learn on the job, we have to learn from our experiences, and we have to create our own magic wand.

You'll create many wands only to find that they do not work for you. You might create one that allows you to get people back for what they did to you. Maybe you'll try and create one that hurts other people the way that you were once hurt. In the end, you'll find your wands will break, are no longer functional, the batteries die, become out of order, and there's no warranty.

You'll see that when you find forgiveness... you really won't hurt anymore.

Forgiving is the best defence against your own emotional pain. It gives you freedom, and only the very strongest, wisest and kindest people can and will choose to forgive.

Additionally, forgiveness is the best medicine you can provide for your physical well-being. According to the Stanford University Centre for Research in Disease Prevention, holding onto bitterness can wear out your immune system and cause damage to your heart. The University of Wisconsin found that those who actually underwent "forgiveness training" showed improvement in the blood flow to their hearts. My very favourite scientific survey was conducted by Dr. Bernie Seigel, a clinical professor of surgery at Yale Medical School. In sharing his findings from fifty-seven patients with well documented "cancer miracles," he explained that these patients decided to let go of their anger and depression, mainly because they just didn't have a lot of time left. After transitioning themselves into a loving state, letting their anger go and reaching out to their loved ones, it was found that their tumors actually started to shrink.

Forgiveness needs to become your magic wand for life.

If you truly believe in an eye for an eye, and feel that you absolutely *must* seek vengeance in order to feel good again. Please allow me to share two very powerful quotes with you:

"An eye for an eye makes the whole world blind."
(MAHATMA GANDHI)

"Forgiveness is the sweetest revenge."

(ISSAC FRIEDMANN)

Apologies and Forgiveness: Can You Have One Without the Other?

The members of the bitter club may have all belonged to the same organization, but they all displayed very different demeanours. Some were angry and cynical, some *appeared* to be happy on first glance, some were competitive, and some were sad. Regardless, they all seemed to be waiting for something. Throughout my mountain climb, I would study them; they fascinated me. They reminded me of those people you see in a restaurant, in the next booth, anxiously looking at their watches every 30 seconds while waiting for their (very obviously) late dinner companion. They fidget, they sigh, and eventually, they stare off into space. Their impatience in what they were waiting for shone crystal clear to me, and piqued my interest. I once apprehensively approached a member of the bitter club. I was scared to death. I told him that I knew what he was waiting for, and asked him what he was planning to do if it never showed up.

If you really want to light a firecracker under someone's ass, bring up the concept of apologies. You'll notice it right away: body posture shifts, facial expressions change, lips purse, and defences run wilder than a fifteen-year-old girl staying out late with her friends for the first time on a Saturday night. There really is something about the concept of these two words that can make people go somewhat batty. So, what is it? What is that "something?"

"It's just an admission of error."

"It makes people feel guilty. That's why they won't say it."

"It's what grown ups do. Not everyone is grown up."

"It shows you a lot about someone's character. I have a whole lot of respect for people who take responsibility when they mess up."

"It saved my marriage."

"It's the weak who can't say I'm sorry. Only people who are strong and confident in themselves say I'm sorry."

"I know some people in my life can say it; and I know people who will never say it."

"Some people say they're just words. But if they are 'just words,' why is it so hard for you to say them?"

"I know people that say it all the time. Then they just make the same mistakes over and over again anyway."

"My wife will just say that 'we think differently'. She'll never just admit she made a mistake."

These are all very interesting and different perspectives. Let me take a few steps back. You see, this section was all neatly planned out, and I was actually really looking forward to writing it because, initially, it was supposed to be one of the easiest sections to write. Basically, I was going to speak about the words "I'm sorry." When they are important, when they are not, what happens when we abuse them and, conversely, what happens when we don't use them enough. Simple enough right? But then, I did something. I went to meet Dr. Monica Vermani for dinner.

Dr. Vermani is a clinical psychologist based in Toronto. Her clinic, the S.T.A.R.T. Clinic for Mood and Anxiety Disorders (Stress, Trauma, Anxiety, Rehabilitation, Treatment) provides treatment services for people who suffer from trauma, mood and anxiety disorders.

Dr. Vermani and I have worked on some writing projects together, but we really didn't know each other from a hole in the wall. The first two hours and three appetizers of our meeting were dedicated to just that. I gravitate to people who want to teach as much as they want to learn; a quality that I find very endearing, and very rare. She taught me some psychological theories that really come in handy when learning about love, letting go of anger, and most importantly, just being happy. As much as I learned from those theories, the real eye-opening moments came about when we discussed the concept of "I'm sorry."

"Well, what does it mean to you?" she asked me as we buttered our bread. She was looking at me kind of funny. I wasn't sure why, but it was evident that she was thinking something. In my enjoyment of the evening, it left my attention that this woman is a trained professional in the workings of the mind. Of course she was thinking something, and for most of the conversation, her thought patterns were always two steps ahead of mine.

I pondered her question: *What does "I'm sorry" mean to me?* I put aside the now cold bread I was just about to eat, and indulged in the hot, steamy bread that our decent-looking waiter just brought to our table. I begin to butter it while thinking of the most sincere answer I could provide. I didn't want to give her a textbook answer. My goal wasn't to impress her with high calibre verbiage; I just wanted to share what genuinely came to my mind as I considered her question. I responded, "It means that someone screwed up, realized it, sincerely felt badly for the pain they caused someone else, and at some point, decided to take responsibility for their actions."

Dr. Vermani took a sip of her wine. "I see," she said. Then, there was silence.

That's it? That's all she had to say? I wait for more to follow, but she didn't say anything. I wait a little longer, pretending that I am completely oblivious to the thick silence that has now filled the air. I wait, and I wait, then I wait some more. Finally, I look up at her and say, "What?"

She smiles at me. "Jessica, I can tell you're an intelligent person." (I instantly feel the same sensation as my nephew after he successfully answers the question, 'What noise does a duck make?')

Dr. Vermani continues, "You've seen quite a bit, and I think you've learned quite a bit. That's great… for you." There was silence again. I can't quite tell if my dinner companion for the evening has just given me a compliment or has told me to wake up and smell the coffee. (I don't even like coffee. I'm more of a tea drinker.) I know now, it was a bit of both, but right then I really didn't know how to respond, and I decided to do what I think is best to do when you feel like you may just not know what you're talking about. I decided to say nothing. I decided to hand the microphone to someone who might just know more than me. It's an interesting concept, one that many have never tried before.

Dr. Vermani spent the next half hour or so speaking to me about the concept of an apology. I listened. I was confused by a lot of what she said at first, but I listened anyway. She didn't preach. She didn't lecture. She just spoke.

Dr. Vermani explained that some people in the world demand it, some just say it to keep peace, sometimes people say "I'm sorry" because it's guilt driven, some use it as a scapegoat. A very small percentage might actually just say it to take accountability for their actions. More often than not, she told me, the apology itself doesn't come from a "pure" place in their hearts. I listened to her, trying to absorb what she said to me. My mind is already racing with questions to ask and statements to clarify, but I could see that she wasn't done yet, and was just getting started. She defined that the words "I'm sorry" suggest that the person in question *did not know* what they were doing when they did it, whatever they did. On the contrary, they knew exactly what they were doing—and they did it anyway. We do the best we can with knowledge that we have, and she repeated the same phrase several times:

> "People do the best they can with the knowledge they have at that time. They were acting based on their previous learning, and who they were at that time. We grow, moment to moment."

She continued, "What's more important is an acceptance of a situation and acceptance of people for who they are. There truly is no need for an 'I'm sorry' when we really believe that their intent was not to be malicious or hurtful."

She maintains that people can change. "Basically, who we were yesterday is not who we are today, and won't be the same as who we are tomorrow. We, as people, are always changing; and, as they say, hindsight is always 20/20."

When she paused, I said, "So basically what you're telling me is that if someone does wrong, they realize it later, they never take accountability for it, and you know it wasn't malicious—then the next step is to just say, "Okay great! Let's go grab a beer!"

"Nope," she said. I'm not saying that at all. I tell her she's making my head hurt, and she laughs. "I never said that people shouldn't take accountability for their own actions," she stated. "It seems that many of us equate the words 'I'm sorry' with accountability, and the truth is that they're not always one in the same; especially when it's being said as a 'scapegoat.'" As the conversation progressed, Dr. Vermani explained that before one can even ask for forgiveness (if they so choose to) you must first take accountability in your own heart. So, before you go out and seek penance from the world, you might just want to admit to yourself that you made a mistake, that you hurt someone else, that you feel badly for that mistake, and that you acknowledge it privately to yourself. And then, you forgive yourself. Just when I thought I was following everything she had just explained, she tagged on, "But not everyone can do that."

"The acknowledgement of a mistake," she proceeded to qualify, "can actually break some people down. Frankly, some people just can't handle it. They can't handle knowing that they've done something that's affected someone else so badly. It eats them up and destroys their ability to function and live on a daily basis. They choose denial because it's easier, and there's nothing you can do to change that except to allow them to walk their own path. You walk yours, let them walk theirs."

We both sip our wine (actually, now we gulp it) and sit back to simmer in the healthy dialogue that has just taken place. Some time passes and Dr. Vermani asks me, "What about the people that don't want an "I'm sorry?"

"I dunno," were the intelligent words that I chose to respond with. She gave me an example that I have put in my own words. A young girl who was molested grows up to become a mother of three. She has a wonderful husband, happy and healthy children, a great career, and is, for all intents and purposes—happy. Ding dong goes the doorbell one day, and there stands the same man who abused her when she was a child. He's old now, and says that he's come to tell her that it took him twenty years to come to terms with what he's done, and that if he could take it all back he would. He says that he's truly sorry and bursts into tears.

"Now what?" asked Dr. Vermani.

I think about it and say, "He's either just given her some much-needed closure, or he's devastated her life, yet again."

"Bingo" she remarked. "He may have just brought back a ton of awful and painful memories that this woman does not want to remember. She doesn't want to think about them, and on the path that she's walked, she's already put these painful memories behind her and dealt with them. This man has now just brought them all back for her to think about and agonize over, all over again."

Dr. Vermani paused for just a moment before she

added, "Oh, and closure? Why do we need to wait for an 'I'm sorry' from someone else before we give ourselves closure? Why does a person need validation from another person to move forward in life? Isn't that an internal process? Why do we need external validation? If you really need that "sorry" to move on, ask yourself why you should be dependent on someone else's words in order for you to feel good again."

Her message is ultimately one of forgiveness for our health, happiness and well-being. The thing is, we're not all built to take accountability in the same way. While some people are very able to look their own faults and past mistakes squarely in the eye, others simply just cannot handle it. It breaks them down. Really acknowledging the pain that they may have inflicted on another human being tears them apart, and paralyzes them.

If someone who has hurt you decides to deliver a heartfelt apology with the intention of accountability, then great! According to Dr. Vermani, this more than likely means that they acted without awareness of the hurt it would cause you. I wonder to myself, just out of curiosity, how would you assess their intentions anyway? Anyone got an "intention measuring scale"? Imagine how much you could sell that for on eBay!

Even if you feel that you deserve an apology, you should never sit around and just wait for it to happen. Waiting anxiously for something that just may never come, will only cause profound damage to your emotions, your heart, and your mind. Closure is something that we must all find within ourselves, regardless of someone else's choice to take or not to take accountability for their own actions. Remember that they did the best they could with the knowledge that they had at that time.

Dr. Vermani says most of us, excluding psychopaths (because they lack a conscience), do not *want* to harm or hurt others. They *learn* behaviours modelled on their parents or other role models in their society. Everything they learn from a very young age becomes their own personal *blueprint*—an interpretation of how the world works in their own minds learned from the influencers in their life.

Everyone is going to do what they need to do to get by. Some will openly acknowledge their mistakes, some will privately acknowledge them, and some have the amazing capability of forgiving themselves quite easily for everything they have ever done (always my favourite kind of people!).

On my drive home I think about the evening I had. Dr. Vermani was right. You don't need an apology to be able to move on. But that being said, you don't need to surround yourself with people who hurt you or make you feel badly either. You walk your path. Let them walk theirs.

Love and forgiveness go hand in hand. You won't be able to reap the benefits of one without practicing the other. Choosing to forgive is choosing to be *better*. Choosing to hold onto a grudge is choosing to be *bitter*, and will hurt no one else but you.

I decide to end the night in the same way that it began: driving home by myself with Sinatra in the background. I ponder what "I'm sorry" means to me. Well, I guess it's like winning the lottery, it would be damn wonderful if I hit the jackpot, but sitting around waiting for it to happen isn't gonna make me rich.

Falling in Love Works Better Than Prozac

In 2007, there were over 2.2 million prescriptions filled for generic brands of Fluoxetine (Prozac) in the United States. I'm not a doctor and don't pretend to know who really needs medication and who doesn't. However, I wish I was able to say that 2.2 million people *fell in love* in 2007 in the United States. If they did, perhaps the prescriptions filled would decrease while our levels of happiness increased.

I told someone my wish. I told them that I wished that all of those people suffering from some form of heartache could fall in love with something and reap the benefits of its healing power. She looked at me similar to the way you're looking at this page right now. Yes, it's kinda corny, kinda sweet, kinda naïve, kinda cute. Some of you may think it's unrealistic for me to believe that love could actually act as a drug. Personally, I think it's one of the most amazing things I have ever learned.

Allow me to explain.

Prozac is a member of SSRI Medications. SSRI stands for: Selective Serotonin Reuptake Inhibitor. Fancy stuff! They are made up of particular compounds that treat depression, mood and anxiety disorders. Other members of the SSRI family include Zoloft, Celexa, Lexapro, and Paxil.

So what is it about Prozac that aids in the treatment of happiness? One of the most common answers seems to point directly at serotonin. Serotonin is a neurotransmitter: a chemical in your brain that assists in the quality of such functions as sleep, appetite, and sex drive. Prozac also targets the brain to create endorphins, your body's natural pain killer. When endorphins are released into your body you are left with an overall feeling of well-being. If your brain does not produce enough neurotransmitters or endorphins, you may become prone to feelings of sadness; and in more severe situations, depression. It's in situations like these that your doctor may decide to write you a prescription to aid in the production of both. You pop the pill, your levels of serotonin and endorphins increase, and you feel somewhat better.

As I researched about the potential benefits of Prozac, something just didn't feel right and I decided to dig deeper. In my research for putting this book together, I found that the benefits of love provide an opportunity to choose *better* over *bitter*. I discovered that when you're focused on something that you absolutely love, your body reacts positively. Prozac and falling in love may be designed to create the same positive effects, except one is a *real* sensation based on *real* life events. The other is just a pill.

Ever heard of Helen Fisher? Her research acts as my pill popper, and increases my levels of serotonin!

On the Internet her name appears on articles about the concept of love as frequently as Tiger Woods's name appears beside the concept of infidelity. Helen Fisher, an anthropology professor at Rutgers University in New Jersey, speaks about some of the benefits of falling in love—with a person.

She explains that there are three stages of love:

1) Lust
2) Attraction
3) Attachment

Each stage is important in its own right, and each stage provides physical and mental health benefits. According to Dr. Fisher, the first stage of lust is driven by sex hormones (testosterone and estrogen). These are the hormones that draw us to desire another person. They are the hormones that make people desire sex, and the benefits of sex are many.

Sex helps you maintain an ideal body weight, and burns approximately 150 calories per half hour, more than yoga or dancing, and the same as weight training or canoeing.

Sex helps to increase blood flow to your brain and to all other organs of your body, making improvements in circulation.

Sex provides the healing power of intimacy. "Sex is good for you, but sex with love is even better," says Dr. Dean Ornish, author of *Love and Survival: the Scientific Basis for the Healing Power of Intimacy*. His research into intimacy and its effects on health have shown how "anything that promotes feelings of love and intimacy is healing. If you have someone who really cares for you and for whom you care in return, someone you are intimately connected with in all ways—emotionally, physically, and spiritually—then you may be three to five times less at risk of premature death and disease from all causes. An open heart can lead to the most joyful and ecstatic sex."

Attraction is the second stage that Dr. Fisher discusses, where you "fall madly in love" as three things increase in your body.

Dopamine: when this is released in your body, you require less sleep, less food, and have increased energy. You might find you are losing your appetite and sleeping less because you are so fixated on this new person that you have found. You're on a rush and a high, and you're feeling sensations of happiness.

Adrenaline/Norepinephrine: when you begin to fall in love with someone, the blood levels of adrenaline in your body increase. For instance, when you get close to your new lover, you get nervous, maybe even a little sweaty, and your heart beats a little quicker.

Serotonin: assists in the quality of sleep, appetite, sex drive, and an overall positive mood.

In the final stage of attachment, scientists predict there may be two major hormones involved. They are

The Bitter Battlefield

oxytocin and vasopressin. Oxytocin is often referred to as the "cuddle hormone," and is released by both genders during orgasm. It promotes bonding among adults, or even a mother to a child. Vasopressin is released after sex, and promotes protection and devotion to your partner.

It seems that falling in love with *something* is not the only miracle worker for your mental and physical health; falling in love with *someone* works just as well. Hmm, bruised, broken 'n' bitter versus better *in love*? Wouldn't that be a great sequel!

Whether you choose to fall in love with something or someone, always remember that it will keep you on the route to better, mentally and physically. And no matter what you hear from the bitter clubs you must always remember, being bitter or better is not your predestined fate. It's your *choice*.

Have you chosen?

Battlefield

Your job here is now complete. You have been given all the tools and resources you will need while out on the battlefield. Remember, your job is to:

Find them: The Bruised, Broken 'n' Bitter Club.
Introduce yourself: The Bruised, Broken 'n' Better Club
Pass on your knowledge of *Falling in Love Works Better Than Prozac!*. Falling in love leads you to *better!*

After months of working on this book I decided it's only right that I go out and celebrate its completion.

Members of the better club and I gather together to head out for a night on the town. We get to our desired venue and, instantly, I feel a strange sensation in my body. It's like I've developed my own personal spidey sense toward the *bitter* and *better*.

It doesn't take long for the alarm bells in my head to go off, and I realize where I am. Unintentionally, I find myself on the battlefield, and you will too. You see, we won't always have the opportunity to prepare for battle. Sometimes, we'll be on our way to run errands, be grabbing a bite to eat or visiting a friend, and we find ourselves in the midst of combat, with no warning.

As members of the better club and I get seated at our table, I realize what I would have done six months ago. All it would have taken was one bitter word from a member of the Stepford Wives club for me to decide that I wasn't interested, and bolt. I wanted nothing to do with their ideologies, their mentalities, and their practices. Today I decide that's not very fair and that I need to practice what I preach. I began this book by explaining that our mission is to stop this *bitter* epidemic from spreading, and I realized that this mission is more than just a one-time fight—it's a lifetime commitment.

I spot them from the corner of my eye. They're watching us. They're about to make their move. We let them; they were just looking for someone to talk to. That's when I hear them, both males and females, speak of their own unique *mountain climb*. I remind my better club members to use their support systems, and to be a support system. I tell them that we must challenge the traditional notion of what bitter "looks like" if we really want to find it, and stop it.

I listen for members of the bitter club to tell me that they're proud of themselves for making it to the top. I anxiously listen for them to say that they got bruised, and then broken, and then broken *again*. I wait for them to tell me that it was the best thing that could have ever happened to them. I coax them to tell me that they've opened the right door and are now walking a *better* path. I wait for them to tell me that they've *fallen in love* with something and how they want to *give back* in their own special and unique way. I don't hear it. I don't hear any of it.

I think of that woman often: the woman from the doctor's waiting room. The same woman who told her doctor that she had "no one to call" after hearing such devastating news. I look at the new group that's just surrounded me and wonder how many of them are in that very same situation.

I let members of the bitter club finish their piece. I'm not concerned. By the end of the night there's no doubt in my mind that they will swap their membership in one club for the other. All it takes is for someone like you and I to extend an arm, an ear... and a little bit of love.

One Final Pet Peeve

Before we part ways, I'd like to clear up a real big pet peeve of mine.

When Patrick Swayze died, the media said that he *lost* his battle with pancreatic cancer. The same was said of the battles fought by Farrah Fawcett, John Wayne, Walt Disney, your next door neighbour, or someone very precious to you in your life....

Every time I hear those words, my blood boils.

Listen up. No one has ever *lost* their battle to cancer. There's no such thing as losing a battle when the fight wasn't a fair one in the first place. Ever heard the expression "sucker punch"? A sucker punch is when someone, very cowardly, decides to throw a jab at you from the side or the rear so that you don't know it's coming. You have no time to plan your defence or your attack. There's no time to strategize, and before you know it, you're knocked off your feet and land on your back with a remarkably hard thud, completely bewildered by what just happened to you. A *fair* fight resembles the exact opposite of this scenario. A fair fight allows you to be completely aware that your opponent is coming, and that they are going to try and hurt you, make you weak, and try to make you fall. A fair fight allows you to practice your absolute right to strategize your next move and think one step ahead. A fair fight allows you to get your fists up so that no one can get away with that cowardly sucker punch.

To all the brave people we have ever known who have died, suffered, or are suffering from cancer: You never lost your battle. Your struggle, your experiences and your bravery just made it easier for the rest of us to battle out our unfair fight. It made it easier for us to be aware of that sucker punch.

You are very courageous.

You are always remembered.

You made us all *better*.